Praise

'Julia Black offers a transformative approach not just to education but to raising families and exploring everyone's potential for creativity. Grounded in research and tested by years of experience, it's a framework for the revolution we need in lifelong learning. As this book explains, anyone can do it!'
— **Philip Ball**, Author of *The Book Of Minds*

'*Lights On Learning* is a transformative guide that taps into the core of what makes every child a passionate, engaged learner. By unveiling the power of a child's innate curiosity and potential, Julia provides parents with the tools to ignite their child's "light", allowing them to thrive and excel not because they have to but because they want to. This book is a game changer for anyone looking to reimagine education as a joyful, self-led adventure, and it empowers families (my own included) to see learning as an opportunity to flourish. A must-read for every parent ready to unlock their child's brilliance.'
— **Fernanda Lind**, CEO and Founder of Rewired Global

'A must-read for parents (and educators). This book offers simple yet powerful neuroscience-informed methods to ignite a love of learning while providing hands-on tools that really work.'
— **Sarah Nykoruk**, Educator, Podcaster, Master Neurocoach

'This book is a must-read for any parent interested in helping their child to switch on their potential for learning. Julia's evidence is compelling; everyone has a natural ability that needs to be unlocked. You need to get started today.'
— **Shonogh Pilgrim**, CEO Whole Education

Lights On Learning

A parent's blueprint for happy, fulfilled, curious kids

Julia Black

Rethink

First published in Great Britain in 2024
by Rethink Press (www.rethinkpress.com)

© Copyright Julia Black

All rights reserved. No part of this publication may be reproduced, stored in or introduced into a retrieval system, or transmitted, in any form, or by any means (electronic, mechanical, photocopying, recording or otherwise) without the prior written permission of the publisher.

The right of Julia Black to be identified as the author of this work has been asserted by her in accordance with the Copyright, Designs and Patents Act 1988.

This book is sold subject to the condition that it shall not, by way of trade or otherwise, be lent, resold, hired out, or otherwise circulated without the publisher's prior consent in any form of binding or cover other than that in which it is published and without a similar condition including this condition being imposed on the subsequent purchaser.

Illustrations © Mel Stephenson 2024

Cover image © Shutterstock | IndriyanSaputra and Listiana1979

*To Mum and Dad, who always believed in me,
even when I failed over and over again.*

*And to Esme and Seb, who kept me going
every time I doubted I could.*

Contents

Introduction	1
PART ONE Connecting Your Circuit	7
1 When The Lights Go Out	9
We all have something we are naturally good at	11
What if disengagement isn't a problem in the first place?	12
'Why can't I help them?'	12
From feeling a failure to the best school report ever	14
Looking at engagement through the Lights Off lens	17
When disengagement turns into chronic stress	20

Too many children are left stumbling in the dark unnecessarily	23
2 Your Lights On And Lights Off Potential	**27**
This is not a soft, fluffy way to learn	28
What does it mean to be Lights Off and Lights On?	29
Your Lights Off state	30
Your Lights On state	31
It is uncomfortable being Lights Off	32
It can be equally uncomfortable being Lights On	33
Don't make the mistake I made for years!	34
What is Lights On Learning?	35
Lights On Learning is available to us all	36
Introducing the Lights On metric	38
What does my data reveal?	40
The Lights On and Lights Off Mindset	41
More than a powerful visual metaphor	43
From anger to feeling invincible	44
Let's get the Lights On metric into your family	46
What does being Lights On and Lights Off mean to you?	47

3 Your Lights On Learning Circuitry	**51**
Your Lights On Learning circuitry	54
Heartset – your emotional connection	55
Mindset – the mental connection	59
Skillset – the physical connection	62
From underperforming to inspired and motivated in less than eight hours	64
4 Flicking The Switch	**69**
Your Heartset is always ready	71
Flicking on your family's switches	74
From rock bottom to award-winning young entrepreneur in less than a year	78
What is it that switches on your family's lights?	79
A new learning adventure opens up	83
PART TWO Getting Wired For Learning	**87**
5 The Lights On Spectrum	**89**
Immersed in radiance	91
Cascading to darkness	92
Your family's Lights On spectrum	94
The essence of each signature	97

	Your unique signatures are key to your child's love of learning	108
	Unpacking the cultural DNA of education	109
6	**Your Lights Off Cascade**	**113**
	Lights Off thoughts are normal	116
	Getting up close and personal with your Lights Off circuits	118
	A few layers deeper	121
7	**Casting Your Lights On Vision**	**125**
	Passion-led learning changes the game	128
	Love in the Lights On spectrum	130
	Having a real love of learning	132
	Coding a vision blueprint for your family	133
PART THREE	**Activating Your Potential**	**145**
8	**Tracking Your Lights On Spectrum**	**147**
	Customise your Lights On spectrum	151
	Getting your family on board	153
	Begin tracking	154
	Intentional daily check-in	158
	Three-day check-in	158

	Your blueprint baseline	160
	Glow or below	161
	The Lights On spectrum is a calibration tool	162
9	**Rewiring Your Lights Off Circuitry**	**165**
	Shining a spotlight on your most limiting beliefs	168
	Set up a daily discipline of metacognition	169
	The situation is neutral	170
	Rewiring your circuitry	171
	Prime in your Lights On circuit	176
10	**Opening Up To Radiance**	**179**
	Cracking your personal code	180
	Radiance is the essence of who we are	181
	Growth spirals	183
	Confronting reality	184
	Radiance is a lifeline	186
	Radiance – an immersion in gratitude	189
	Your inner-smile memories	191
	Activate your Lights On state	191
	Create an inner-smile memory bank	193
	Future-proofing your family	194

11 Calibrating For Success	**197**
Why am I here? Because I am	198
When you shine, your family can, too	199
From fearful to unstoppable writer in less than six months	203
Conclusion	**211**
Lights On Learning is an inner game anyone can play	211
Acknowledgements	**217**
The Author	**223**

Introduction

When you find that 'thing' your child is born to explore, everything changes. I call it their switch, and you see it in their eyes – it is like their lights have come on. When you bring your child's passions and superpowers into the equation, you will see them become highly engaged learners, superfast. As they claim their place in the spotlight, they shine with radiance. Lights On! When things get hard or they face a challenge, they do not give up. They dig in. They find a way to achieve at the most extraordinary level. Not because they have to, but because they want to. This is the game changer. They will want to quit, at times, of course they will, but they won't. All because of you!

This book distils two decades' of learning alongside thousands of children, young people and their parents. I've been obsessive about understanding the art and science of learning and how we can fully express our human potential in a sustainable, healthy and inspiring way. The exciting news is that no matter how disengaged your child is, you are the best person to switch on their love for learning, regardless of their age or how their brains are beautifully wired.

My adventure began as a Parent Governor and Chair of the Parent Teacher Association of my children's school. In 2010, we won an award for 'Changing the Life of the School' from the National Council of Parent Teachers Associations. Three years later, I set up a creative learning centre called Explorium. We ran sessions for home-educating families, flexischoolers, and after-school and holiday clubs, and we collaborated with over fifteen local schools. Working with so many children, neurotypical and neurodiverse, from age four to early adulthood, I saw what worked and what didn't work. I noticed patterns. As a result, I created my own educational philosophy, approach and blueprint – Lights On® Learning – which connects us mentally, emotionally and physically to learning, so we can flourish as passionate, self-led learners.

I discovered that the culture of learning in the family home has the biggest impact on a child's attitude to learning. Parents were unconsciously getting in the way of their children's learning and growth, unaware they were stuck in an old-school educational paradigm. The narrative that the education system is

INTRODUCTION

broken leads us to believe disengagement is a problem to solve. It isn't. Instead of a global learning crisis, as identified by the World Bank, UNICEF and UNESCO, I believe we face a global learning opportunity of epic scale.[1]

As parents, we make a lot of mistakes. It comes with the role. My book isn't about blaming or shaming you, but rather inviting you into a new paradigm. We all have this incredible technology – our hearts, brains and bodies – that enables us to be incredible learners. It is the power of our minds, the neuroplasticity of our brains, the intuition from our hearts, and the capacity to feel within our bodies, that enables us to unlock and express our human potential at an extraordinary level.

There is something magical about the embodied experience of exploring your potential. Knowing how to switch on your creative energy, activate your learning circuitry and supercharge your inner power takes courage and commitment. It requires you to connect with your thoughts and emotions and take ownership of your actions and outcomes.

My approach to education doesn't require you to step away from traditional education to transform your child's mental, emotional and physical connection to

---

[1] World Bank Group, *The State of Global Learning Poverty: 2022 update* (2022), www.worldbank.org/en/topic/education/publication/state-of-global-learning-poverty, accessed 2 September 2024

learning. Without anything needing to change externally, everything can shift internally and their experience of the world around them will change. I hope my book encourages you to flex, enhance, enrich and extend your child's education adventure, as I have done for my two, and thousands of others.

To help you get a feel for Lights On Learning, I share personal stories, include simple activities and pose questions for you to explore. I also introduce you to my most powerful tool, the Lights On spectrum, intending to offer you fresh insights to spark new conversations within your family and beyond. With their permission, I also include insights, wisdom and quotes from children and parents. It is thanks to their courageous vulnerability to work with me that Lights On Learning is ready to transform families, schools and communities around the world.

My vision is of a world in which all children love learning. Children who love learning can, and will, change the world, and working directly with you, as the parent or primary carer, is the fastest way to achieve this reality. This book is written with love for you, the parent with a sparky, brilliant family who is hungry to learn with compassion, courage and curiosity. Whatever your story has been until this point, we're going to create magic together! Time to open the portal and let your Lights On Learning adventure unfold.

INTRODUCTION

BONUS MATERIAL

To receive a bonus workbook and audio recording of my Lights On Activation scan the QR code below or go to

www.lightsonuniverse.com/bookbonus

PART ONE
CONNECTING YOUR CIRCUIT

1
When The Lights Go Out

When my daughter was three years old, I went to pick her up from preschool. The owner, Claire, asked if she could have a word. Esme had been unusually defiant. She had run towards the road and refused to stop. When they called her, she turned, smiled and kept running.

'OK, it's one of those conversations!' I thought.

My dyslexic father had notoriously been the naughtiest boy in his school, so I thought to myself, 'She's got his maverick gene. Buckle up for the ride.' What Claire said next surprised me.

'She's bored. I think we need to teach her to read.'

Esme was young, but like all children, she wanted to run, skip, hop and jump her way through learning. Claire recognised that. Instead of clamping down on her behaviour, her team raised their game so that Esme could flourish.

Unfortunately, millions of children around the world don't have a 'Claire' in their lives. They lack a teacher who sees them for who they are: hungry and curious to learn. Sparky. Brilliant. Full of radiance and joy. A bundle of creative energy looking for opportunities to express themselves fully.

When I think about my educational career, not one teacher witnessed 'me' or saw my essence. Luckily for me, my father, who graduated from naughtiest boy to rebel with a cause, was my mentor. He understood my potential for greatness, as he did for many others, too. I always felt his absolute belief in me. Even when I failed over and over again, he'd simply say 'Keep going, sweetie. Persist, persist, persist.' He had an energy of certainty. That no matter what, everything would be OK.

What about you?

Did you have someone who believed in you?

I hope you did, but if you didn't, then everything is about to change. I share my father's gift to see the brilliance in people. I see where they naturally shine. It has become my life's work to pass this superpower on to families like yours.

With Artificial Intelligence (AI) 'set to be a billion times smarter than us',[2] it is time to reconnect with our unique human spirit. Using the art and science of learning, there's never been a better time to explore our potential in a new, sustainable way. To lead our children to learn what they love so that they can love what they learn starts with one simple premise.

We all have something we are naturally good at

When you learn through your passions, you become more courageous and willing to take risks. You still experience fear and cascade into darkness at times, but you learn to harness the inner power within your shadows. Guided by your own internal light, you grow in new, expansive and exponential ways. I've found that children who lead themselves through passion-led projects naturally include a level of challenge that pushes them beyond their comfort zone and skill level. They learn to ask for support when they need it, and how to collaborate with others to plug the gaps in their skills.

---

[2] M Gawdat, *SCARY SMART: the future of artificial intelligence and how you can save our world* (Bluebird, 2022)

To arrive at this point, of having a happy, engaged, self-led learner, you may first need to change your relationship with disengagement.

What if disengagement isn't a problem in the first place?

When you think about a child being disengaged, what images spring to mind?

Head in hands. Slumped in their chair. Scrolling mindlessly on their phones. Locking themselves in the bathroom, complaining of stomach aches and refusing to go to school. Perhaps they are being disruptive. Rude. Enrolling others to behave 'badly' with them. Maybe you see compliance. Pleasing everyone else, yet no longer seeming to care about anything.

Through this lens, it is easy to judge what you see and to focus on their behaviour. After all, it's frustrating they're wasting so much potential. Anyone living or working with a disengaged child, teen or adult will undoubtedly at some point feel they are failing.

'Why can't I help them?'

That's when you begin your search for solutions and find plenty who will tell you what is wrong with your child.

WHEN THE LIGHTS GO OUT

What is wrong with me?

My starting point, with everyone I work with, is to assume that nothing is wrong with them.

Is your child happy and engaged when they are doing something they love? Yes or no?

Are they sparkier on the weekends, during the holidays or in after-school clubs? Yes or no?

Are they actively telling you they are bored, hate school, or find your home education dull (ouch!)? Yes or no?

If your answer is yes to all of these, you're probably looking at a normal healthy reaction to being bored and disconnected from learning. We can turn this around fast. If the answers are no, and they're disengaged across the board, you might want to investigate further, but not before you've tried to ignite that hint of a spark, as I did for Ollie.

From feeling a failure to the best school report ever

I met Ollie when he was thirteen years old.

'The person I want to be has never made it into school,' he told me.

Since age five, he had felt like a failure, that he was stupid. He didn't believe he would achieve anything in his life: 'How far have I got in eight years? At the end of every day I go home with this negativity. The information is hidden in this huge web which I'm trying to unpick extremely slowly.'

As his mum, Sandra, said, 'Everyone focused on what was wrong with Ollie.'

Let's do the maths. That's roughly 10,000 hours of having Special Educational Needs and feeling worthless. Shockingly, we accept this reality for so many children. When we judge a child by what they can't do, they become disempowered. As nothing seems to work, they feel 'what's the point?'

Apathy takes hold, mental wellbeing suffers and they lose their appetite to learn. Before we know it, that light in our sparky kids, like Esme and Ollie, has dimmed.

Let's try a different strategy. If everyone has something they are naturally good at, we need to look for what switches on their lights. Then we turn the dial right up and support them to cope when their lights dim or go out.

I found the 'switch' to Ollie's creative energy within minutes. He was a natural-born visual creator and storyteller. As he began expressing his ideas through filmmaking, photography and animation, he transformed as a learner. Immediately. His teachers noticed a difference in the classroom, too, as his principal shared:

> 'Ollie is so much more visible within the school and more engaged in lessons. He is now part of the class and has found a way to engage with school and be Ollie.'[3]

That academic year, Ollie received his best school report ever. Of course he did.

When Ollie felt safe, seen and heard, he became courageous enough to express his authentic self across the board. Lights On. With two hours a week

---

3   Watch the interview here: https://youtu.be/cLRBIdDHBkM?si=pCd6z8oO_rAKU8jX

progressing his passion projects, Ollie shifted gears. He embraced his neurodiverse brain, tuned into his creative energy, took intentional action and got different outcomes.

Because Ollie had been disengaged for a prolonged period, he had unplugged his inner power. As he reconnected his heart, grew his mindset and developed passion-related skills, his potential unfolded with ease. By switching his creative energy back on, which is a simple process, he took full ownership and ran with it. A small shift that gave him tangible evidence of his true capabilities had a profound impact on his confidence and ability to learn. Essentially, he started to believe in himself again.

> 'I've gone from thinking everything about me is rubbish. That I'm never going to have a life, to being good at something and having that drive. The change has been extreme. I'm a different person. I have the confidence to do whatever I want. I'm trying hard in lessons. My creative mindset has impacted on everything.'[4]

Esme, age three, and Ollie, age thirteen, gave clear behavioural signals that they were disengaging. The difference is that Esme's teacher saw it as a growth opportunity, but for Ollie, it was a problem to fix. For eight long years! The common thread is that, when

---

4   Watch the interview here: https://youtu.be/zkppwPoTrNU?si=fC4JNMFC4jqTSeex

both were allowed to express their authentic selves, their engagement shifted instantly. Or, as I would say, with a flick of a switch.

From Lights Off to Lights On.

Looking at engagement through the Lights Off lens

To understand disengagement in a new light (pun intended!), let's look at the words children, young people and adults have used to describe how it feels when they are, what I call, feeling Lights Off:

- Lonely
- Disconnected
- Scared
- Frustrated
- Angry
- Apathetic
- Bored

If you think about your child feeling this way rather than seeing them as disengaged, how does that change how you feel towards them? When parents and teachers I work with see a child as Lights Off, they immediately move out of judgement and into compassion. Rather than punish them for their behaviour, or force them to sit for three hours to do a ten-minute homework, they know the child feels scared, lost and disconnected from the learning process. Disconnected from their own brilliance. Disconnected from their innate passion to be the explorer, artist, scientist, mathematician, filmmaker or inventor they were born to be.

When children stop learning, for whatever reason, it is an extremely uncomfortable place for them to be. Through this lens, it is clear that, when a child has these negative thoughts and feelings, disengagement is a normal and healthy reaction. It is a clear signal that their stress response has been triggered. As the Yerkes-Dobson curve shows below, we need a certain level of stress, or arousal, to perform at our best. To be Lights On.[5]

Too little and we become bored or complacent. Lights Dim. The work is too easy so we switch off. 'What's the point? I know this already. It's so boring.' Too much stress, or distress, affects our ability to perform even the simplest of tasks. Lights Off.

---

5   RM Yerkes and JD Dodson, 'The relation of strength of stimulus to rapidity of habit-formation', *Journal of Comparative Neurology and Psychology*, 18/5 (1908), 459–482, https://doi.org/10.1002/cne.920180503

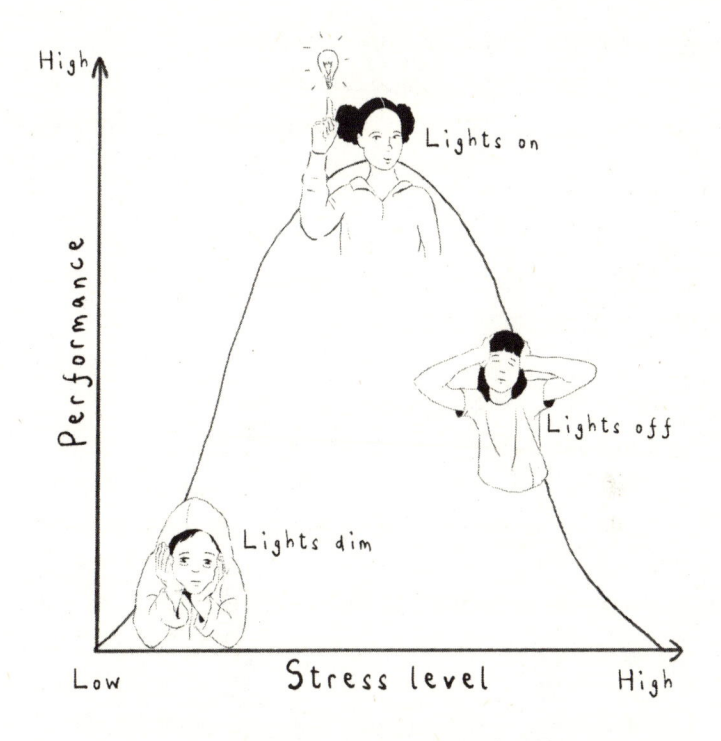

A graph showing Performance (y-axis, Low to High) versus Stress level (x-axis, Low to High) as an inverted-U curve. Three figures are marked along the curve: "Lights dim" at low stress/low performance, "Lights on" at the peak (a figure pointing up to a lit lightbulb), and "Lights off" on the descending side at high stress (a figure covering their ears).

Understanding how to use our stress response for learning is hugely important, for us as parents and for our children. Opportunities and challenges that lead to eustress, or optimal stress, help us understand how our body's stress response feels. The release of hormones, like adrenaline and noradrenaline, will give us a burst of energy and heightened alertness. Our heart rate increases to pump more blood through to our body, and our breathing will get faster and deeper to send more oxygen to our muscles. When we understand that these are useful signals for learning and that they are normal, healthy responses to the challenges we face, we build mental and emotional resilience. Importantly, we also experience the joy of post-struggle success when we achieve something despite the challenges we faced.

When disengagement turns into chronic stress

When we are too quick to label something wrong with a disengaged child we create a problem that doesn't necessarily exist. Their ability to manage stress and regulate their nervous system can be compromised and everyday stress triggers that come with learning in a school setting, or at home, may begin to feel overwhelming.

Dr Sarah McKay's bio-psycho-social model, Bottom-Up, Top-Down, Outside-In, is a useful framework to explore how disengagement can lead to a bigger problem if we misread the clear signal a child gives us.[6]

Let's start with the Outside-In factors. These are elements outside of us which we pick up through our senses, in this case, what we see and hear from others around us, such as finger-pointing and judgement. A child may see, hear or sense their parent's frustration, disappointment or anxiety that something is wrong. Teachers' reports reveal they're falling behind or under performing and tell them, 'If you don't do

---

6   S McKay, *Demystifying The Female Brain* (Hachette UK, 2018)

Overwhelm
I give up
I can't do it
depression
frustration
stress
fear
cortisol
Lazy
panic
anger
Failure
You're a disappointment
I'm not enough

well in school, you won't find a good job.' Yet influencers and entrepreneurs in social media are everywhere saying that school does not set us up for success in the real world.

The Bottom-Up factors in McKay's model relate to our biology. If a child's disengagement is not understood or it is seen as a problem to fix within the child, the internal source of the stress may not be resolved. School becomes a threatening place to be, and it doesn't feel good to be there. This can lead to chronic activation of the child's stress-response system (hypothalamic-pituitary-adrenal axis) and you are likely to start to see school refusal. With no respite from the external and internal stressors, the amygdala will continue to trigger a cascade of physiological responses, which affects their decision-making, learning and memory, which makes it challenging to focus, learn and grow.[7]

The Top-Down factors include our conscious thoughts, emotions, personality, language, expectations and belief systems. As a child begins to have negative thoughts and emotions around learning they feel scared, angry, anxious or depressed. This impacts their ability to regulate their emotions, and a negative loop of thoughts and feelings creates a sense of shame, guilt or embarrassment which affects their

---

7   Center on the Developing Child, 'Toxic stress' (Harvard University, 2015), https://developingchild.harvard.edu/science/key-concepts/toxic-stress, accessed 22 August

neurobiology and neurochemistry, and also impacts their self-belief, confidence and identity as a learner. This self-fulfilling prophecy – they believe they can't, and so they can't – dims their light even more as their mental, emotional and physical health begins to suffer as a result of being switched off to learning.

It's exhausting even thinking about disengagement through this model! Where do we begin to solve it? Viewing disengagement through the lens of being Lights Off makes the solution so much simpler. Find what switches on their lights. Spark their curiosity. Power up their creative energy and switch their full beams back on. We no longer have a problem to solve but an enormous opportunity on our hands. How exciting.

Too many children are left stumbling in the dark unnecessarily

Millions of children around the world, like Ollie, are being labelled as 'failures' throughout their entire educational careers. The World Bank, UNESCO and UNICEF have declared that since Covid-19 the global learning crisis has got worse, with only one-third of ten-year-olds globally being able to read a simple text.[8]

---

8   The World Bank, *The State of Global Learning Poverty: 2022 update* (The World Bank, 2022), https://thedocs.worldbank.org/en/doc/e52f55322528903b27f1b7e61238e416-0200022022/original/Learning-poverty-report-2022-06-21-final-V7-0-conferenceEdition.pdf, accessed 22 August 2024

This is because the old-school paradigm asks children to leave their curiosities, passions and natural-born talents outside the school gates:

> 'For the next fourteen years, you will put aside what you love to do more than anything in the world. That talent, gift and superpower you have, we're not interested in that. Forget it! Now sit down and focus on your phonics!'

OK, I'm intentionally being provocative here, but I do feel that one day soon we will look back and say, 'What were we thinking?' When we ask children to put their authentic selves to one side and ignore what is in their hearts, what are we saying to them?

> 'When it's genuinely five days a week, six hours a day and I'm doing nothing because I don't understand it, it's a waste of time. It destroys my confidence. It makes me feel like we don't matter. That's the feeling I have at the end of every day and I go home with this negativity. It's like the person who wants to do stuff, to have the chance to do everything, hasn't made an appearance at school. It's not an ideal day for anyone.' (Ollie)

There you have it: it makes them feel like they don't matter. When a child trusts that you will actively listen and do something about it, they will be honest. It isn't just those who are struggling academically who feel like this. It is also the 'A-graders', like my daughter. Here's what she shared ten years later, after that fateful day at preschool:

> 'The school system doesn't make you feel good about yourself. You are either doing well but it doesn't matter. Or you're not doing well and you feel really bad about yourself. I kind of feel empty. When you're in a lesson, you sit and look at the clock and it's going slowly. You're listening to the teacher talk about something that you don't care about, and it's just like… Really? Come on!
>
> 'I want to feel excited by what I'm learning. Something that matters to me. Something that develops my strengths. I want to be independent, creative, problem solving. I want to be unique; I don't want to be the same as everyone else. Everyone has different qualities that will contribute to different things in the world. What's really important is we don't lose them.'

I naively assumed that, because Esme doesn't have the neurodiversity that runs in my family, she would thrive in school. I've since worked with many neurotypical high achievers who feel that who they are doesn't matter. Their role is to show up, do what the teacher asks and get the grades to keep their parents happy and proud. This is not high engagement. It is compliance. When we cap our children's learning with old-school thinking, a prescribed curriculum and standardised metrics, we ignore the richness of being human. This doesn't serve anyone, particularly in the age of generative AI, which can outperform our children on many tasks. It certainly does not serve the future of humanity to systematically disconnect children from their authentic creative spirit at such a young age.

In the next chapter, we're going to explore in more detail what it means to be Lights Off and Lights On so you don't continue to make mistakes that are easily avoided. I will also introduce you to my simple metric so you can turn your child's disengagement into a growth opportunity.

2
Your Lights On And Lights Off Potential

When my son, Seb, was nine years old, he walked up to me with a big smile on his face.

'Mum,' he said, 'I am really loving being me at the moment.'

Lights On!

It is one of my inner-smile memories, supercharged with love, and I will cherish it forever. From age seven, he had shown a natural talent for filmmaking. He would instinctively trim shots by one or two frames to make a smoother edit.

By age nine, his digital literacy was so strong that the teenagers in my creative learning centre would call out, 'Where's Seb? I need his help!' This grew his social skills massively.

At age eleven, he was making films for my business, charities and entrepreneurs. He had his own online course, Digital Directors and a Special FX Hitfilms tutorial YouTube channel. Seb's 'digital wizardry switch' was well and truly on and he could use frustrations, obstacles and blocks in a healthy way to find solutions.

As a parent, it is exciting to see your child lead their learning at this level. It's what I want for your family. When children learn what they love and love what they learn, they naturally tune into being Lights On. Powered by emotions such as love, gratitude and joy, they explore harmoniously with their head, heart and hands aligned. They become self-motivated creators guided by a strong sense of passion and purpose.

This is not a soft, fluffy way to learn

It takes courageous vulnerability for a child to express what is in their heart and mind. Motivated by their curiosity, they will step beyond the edges of their current abilities into the unknown. This is where being Lights Off becomes a normal and healthy part of the learning process. It is incredibly challenging to become great at something you feel passionate about. So many of us give up on our dreams and brilliance early on because, when we tune into our natural gifts, we face increasing levels of challenge, more frequent failure and seemingly insurmountable obstacles to success. It's natural to feel frustrated, vulnerable, angry and even fearful at times, that's part of learning, but it feels emotionally uncomfortable. In this deep learning terrain, the pull to give up becomes stronger over time as our inner self-talk gets louder and more negative. Whether we quit or keep going will depend on how we respond when Lights Off. This will ultimately be what defines us as a learner and determines what we can achieve in life.

What does it mean to be Lights Off and Lights On?

Being Lights Off and Lights On refers to your mental, emotional, physical and spiritual state of being. It is what you are thinking, feeling and how you act at any given moment. Your thoughts and emotions determine your actions, which affect your outcomes and influence how you experience the world.

Thoughts + Emotions + Actions = Outcomes

Just as quickly as you can become Lights Off, you can flick the switch into being Lights On. Toddlers are a great example of this with their huge tantrums followed by smiles, laughter and cuddles.

LIGHTS ON LEARNING

Your Lights Off state

Being Lights Off is a reactive state. Your thoughts limit and diminish your power. 'I can't do this. It's too hard. I'll never be successful, so why bother? I might as well give up now.' Everything feels hard, pointless, forced and challenging. Parents have described it as walking through treacle, and they feel insecure, anxious and under threat in some way.

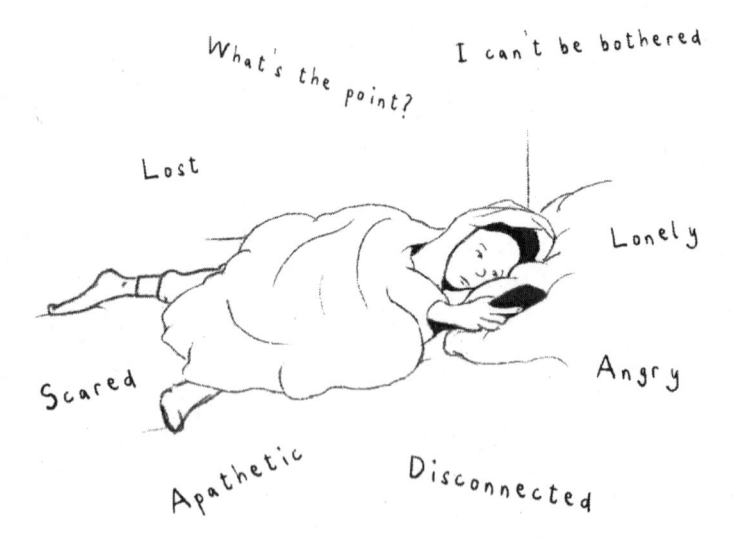

What's the point? I can't be bothered Lost Lonely Scared Angry Apathetic Disconnected

Being Lights Off can be a sad, fearful and lonely place because you carry around an energetic heaviness that leaves others feeling deflated, too. Your negative thoughts lead you deep into the darkest recesses of your mind where you feel there is something deeply wrong with you. No matter what you do, nothing makes a difference. You'll never achieve anything, let alone your dreams, so you don't take action. You procrastinate, and step into overwhelm and get busy with distractions. You become tired, disconnected from the world around you, more inward-focused, narrow-minded and self-absorbed. You may also feel a lot of shame, embarrassment or humiliation, which leads you to feel socially isolated, and dims your light even more. If you are Lights Off for too long, your mental, emotional and physical health will, of course, suffer.

Your Lights On state

In contrast, when you are Lights On, your energy is warm, welcoming and inspiring. People see it in your eyes and feel it in your presence. Your thought patterns are empowered. 'I can do this. I have what it takes to keep going, no matter what.' Emotions such as contentment, hope, happiness, love, joy, peace, awe and gratitude make you feel alive. Like you can do anything. You are more creative and energised when you are Lights On and have a rock-solid belief in yourself and a positive sense of wellbeing. You like who you are.

When you are Lights On, you are fully in creation mode, expressing yourself clearly, feeling authentic and inspired to take action.

I can do it *Joy* *Flow* *Passion* *Love* *I am awesome* *Freedom*

It is uncomfortable being Lights Off

Parents often say 'My child gets so frustrated when they can't do something.' Yep! That's learning for you. Take a moment to reflect on how you think, feel and act when your child becomes Lights Off. Because there's no doubt it is emotionally uncomfortable to be Lights Off ourselves, and even more painful to see our children's lights dim.

What is your go-to solution when they make a mistake or fail to achieve something? Do you step in and desperately try to show them they 'can' by taking over? Or do you allow them to try, fail and try again, as my parents did? Maybe you console them and divert their attention to something more fun to get them happy again.

Helping your child navigate within the dark to switch their lights back on will be the biggest gift you can give them. Having greater awareness of how their mental, emotional and physical state of being affects the decisions they make, and outcomes they achieve, will enable them to grow as a learner.

What needs to change for you to sit in the dark, momentarily alongside them, so they can learn the wisdom and insights that come from their Lights Off state?

It can be equally uncomfortable being Lights On

What has surprised me is how equally uncomfortable it can be to shine at our brightest. Some of us learn early on in life not to shine too brightly or to cast a shadow over someone else's brilliance. 'Tone it down a notch. You're too much.' Foreboding joy, which Brené Brown talks about in her work on vulnerability, has repeatedly come up as an obstacle to being Lights On within my global community of parents.[9] The fear of losing what feels 'too good to be true' means we lower our expectations and don't ask for much in the first place. We settle. Not Lisa, one inspiring mum

---

9   B Brown, *Daring Greatly: How the courage to be vulnerable transforms the way we live, love, parent and lead* (Penguin Random House Audio Publishing Group, 2012)

I worked closely with who strived to reach a point where she shone brightly so her son could too.

'My lights are on so full right now I could light up Wembley Stadium.'

Yes! That is what we are aiming for. When you shine fully, your family will too, even when they have moments of being Lights Off.

Don't make the mistake I made for years!

For a long time, I assumed we wanted to avoid being Lights Off. I believed it was a negative state to be in. I now know differently. Being Lights On is not an end destination you arrive at. Bing! Lights On forever! That would severely limit your experience of being human. Lights Off is hugely important for our growth as learners, and the more opportunities your family has to move fluidly between Lights On and Lights Off, the more resilient they will become. The problem arises when we become stuck in the darkness of the Lights Off state and rarely step into the light.

We give Lights Off emotions such as anger, frustration, loneliness and sadness so much negative meaning and judge ourselves harshly when we feel them. Once aware of their crucial role in our learning and growth, we can view them with compassion. From now on, think of your Lights Off state as uncomfortable, maybe even painful at times, rather than negative. Because when it comes to learning, your Lights Off state is key to your growth. As Jo, a mum of two and my right-hand woman in business, so wisely put it: 'While you can't learn if you are Lights Off all the time, you also can't maximise your growth if your lights are always on.' When your family knows how to journey through the light and dark spaces of their internal learning landscape, the full magic of Lights On Learning comes into play.

What is Lights On Learning?

Lights On Learning is an inside-out philosophy and passion-led educational approach that recognises your mental, emotional and physical states are key to optimising your family's human potential. Learning in this way is very much a whole-body experience: if you are not feeling it, you are probably not engaged in it.

Lights On Learning is less about what you learn, where you learn, or even how you learn, and all about who you are being as a learner. When your child realises that they have a choice about what they think, how they feel and the results they can achieve in life, it transforms their educational experience. Simply knowing their Lights Off state is a signal that growth is around the corner, enables them to become more courageous, resilient and intrinsically motivated learners. As your family learns that success is an inner game, they can enter the realm of exponential growth with ease and flow.

Lights On Learning is available to us all

Lights On Learning is designed around one equitable fact – we all have the inbuilt ability to shine. Once we learn to switch on our inner power, we can dial it up to whatever intensity we choose. I have worked with neurotypical and neurodiverse children and families and apply the same principles and use the same tools and strategies.[10] Here are two accounts from mothers within my community, who relate how it works for them:

> 'With neurodiversity firmly in the mix, Lights On Learning frees you from looking for a fix. You stop looking for the problems you are constantly told to do through the Special Educational Needs system (SEND). You start looking for their brilliance instead. We were on the SEND path from preschool as my daughter had an amazing quirky personality from an early age, so I trod a tricky parenting path of how to help her fit in without squashing

---

10 The Brain Charity, 'Neurodivergent, neurodiversity and neurotypical: a guide to the terms' (2022), www.thebraincharity.org.uk/neurodivergent-neurodiversity-neurotypical-explained/, accessed 24 August 2024

her spirit. However, I was always looking to protect her, being told she was different or "special", in that not-so-helpful way.

'We were advised to get a diagnosis to secure help, so we did. However, all that gave us was a label. Autism. It did not describe the amazing child she was. Having been involved with Lights On Learning, I was able to advocate in a new way. I looked for a school where she could be herself and had a flexi-school agreement to give her one day at home each week.' (Jo)

A message from a mother of a neurotypical family:

'Being a neurotypical family means we know how to tick the boxes in education. However, this is only scratching the surface of what learning is. It only invites a small part of us to grow. Learning to be a Lights On learner as an adult has opened up a whole different world for me, that I never knew I could be a player in. I understand what strengths and gifts I can bring to the world, and I know what it takes to be able to live that life. For my family to be able to understand who they are, and what they love doing and go after it, no matter what, is the ultimate gift. Who wouldn't want that for their kids?

'This is not just for my children, this is for my grandchildren, great-grandchildren and on. Once you have this in your family culture, it can be passed down through generations. Lights On Learning allows us to learn in any environment, and allows the whole of us to grow, with our health as a whole; mind, body and spirit. It is so much more than an educational model. It's a way of being human, with a love of learning.' (Felicity)

However your family's brains are (beautifully) wired, I hope this reassures you that you can create a culture of Lights On Learning in your home and foster trust, connection, playfulness and creativity. Let's dive in and make this personal and relevant for your family, so you can begin the process of getting them loving learning again.

Introducing the Lights On metric

We live in an age where burnout, stress and poor mental ill-health are real for so many of us. NHS UK statistics in 2023 reveal that one in five children and young people aged eight to twenty-five years have a probable mental disorder.[11] I've never been prepared

---

11 NHS England, 'One in five children and young people had a probable mental disorder in 2023' (2023), www.england.nhs.uk/2023/11/one-in-five-children-and-young-people-had-a-probable-mental-disorder-in-2023/, accessed 25 August 2024

to trade the mental health of a child for any grade, and I don't believe you should either. Therefore, I've created my own Lights On metric which changes the educational game.

Lightbulb diagram containing two columns of words:

Left column (Lights Off): Bored, Frustrated, Annoyed, On Edge, Uninspired, Impatient, Distant, Apathetic, Tetchy, Stuck, Tired, Low

Right column (Lights On): Vibrant, Awesome, Excited, Aligned, Confident, Satisfied, Productive, Energised, Unconstrained, High energy, Forward looking, Full of passion

My Lights On metric is an internal measure of your mental, emotional and physical connection to learning. It highlights a child's readiness to learn and grow by recognising that their power to achieve comes from within. Old-school assessments with their arbitrary milestones judge children like Esme, Ollie and Seb against a standard measure of success. This creates a hierarchy of achievement and a glass ceiling over their learning. Tell a child they are struggling to read, falling behind or are continually failing and guess what? They will believe you!

Lights On Learning gives children back ownership over their learning, growth and outcomes. It ensures they get plenty of tangible evidence of what they can do, so they will be hungry to unlock new levels of potential, over and over again. Every child is capable of achieving extraordinary outcomes, and the simplicity of my metric means you, as a parent, can use it as a tool for growth.

What does my data reveal?

The binary nature of my Lights On metric makes it highly effective to get headline data. It allows you to ask your child how they feel about their time in school, or their home education, in a neutral way.

When I asked a group of Year 8 students to tell us anonymously whether they felt more Lights On or Lights Off for the majority of their time in school, the results were split. Fifty-two per cent of eighty-four students declared being Lights On. Forty-eight per cent were mainly Lights Off. This clearly showed the level of disconnection that was happening to them daily.

When I asked a group of head teachers how many children they felt were Lights Off in their schools, they said:

'About a third,' said one.

'It's more than that,' another one said.

'It's definitely more than that,' said another.

My own anecdotal findings are backed up by large studies by Yale researchers who surveyed 21,678 students. They found that 75% felt 'tired, bored or stressed' by their education.[12]

I think we can say with certainty that children and young people around the world are not shining as brightly as they could be. This needs to change, and Lights On Learning is the approach to make that paradigm shift happen.

The Lights On and Lights Off Mindset

To anchor this in, let's look at the stark contrast between how we perceive the world when we look through a Lights Off versus Lights On lens.

---

[12] J Moeller, MA Brackett, Z Ivcevic, AE White, 'High school students' feelings: Discoveries from a large national survey and an experience sampling study', *Learning and Instruction* (April 2020), www.sciencedirect.com/science/article/abs/pii/S0959475218304444, accessed October 2024

Lights Off	Lights On
You see a world full of problems and make decisions from a place of scarcity.	You see a world of solutions and make decisions from a place of abundance.
You hang out with guilt, shame, anxiety and inaction.	You tap into curiosity, creativity, excitement and action.
You have to push, force and drag yourself to do something. You take action from a sense of obligation, regret or fear of what might happen if you don't.	Your vision pulls you forward into action with compassion. You find meaning through self-expression and contributing positively to the world around you.
It is difficult to see even the smallest of wins, let alone the lessons to be gained.	The biggest failure can be viewed as a win because of what you learn from it.
You are often unhappy, discontented and unfulfilled, no matter what you achieve.	You feel happy, content and fulfilled, even when it takes time to achieve your goals.
You feel unsafe, fearful and on high alert for threats.	You feel a sense of peace, freedom and profound gratitude.

When you look at this contrast, which lens do you feel you look through more? If you are living predominantly with a Lights Off mindset, you will focus on the lack within your life. In contrast, your Lights On mindset enables you to see the richness in your everyday life and opens you up to abundance, gratitude and love.

Lights On Learning is intentionally designed to stack Lights On experiences in your favour. Barbara

Fredrickson's scientific research on positive emotions shows us that for every negative experience we have, we want to make sure we have three positive ones. She calls this the positivity ratio of 3:1, which she has discovered is the tipping point for humans to flourish.[13] Lights On Learning builds in what she refers to as a positivity resonance, so you are Lights On more often and for longer periods, not with a 'smile and think positive thoughts' strategy, but as an internal rewiring job.

More than a powerful visual metaphor

Back in 2016, when I first developed my Lights On and Lights Off metric,[14] it was a metaphor based on my intuition and practical discoveries. A way for me to know when my team was getting it right. You see it in their eyes; it's like their lights have come on. However, as I learned about our neurobiology, neurochemistry, heart coherence and energetics, the more sense it made to learn to be Lights On through choice, not circumstance. It is within the Lights On state that I have discovered we access our exponential potential. The more I tuned into peak performance and creative flow for myself and families in my global community, the more I understood the importance and power of being both Lights On and

---

13 B Fredrickson, *Love 2.0: Creating happiness and health in moments of connection* (Plume, 2014)
14 J Black, 'Lights On: The question I would ask you is: Should our children journey through 14 years of education with their lights on or off?', *Lights On!* (February 2017), 10–11, https://issuu.com/explorium/docs/lights_on, accessed 17 September 2024

Lights Off. It is within our Lights Off state we unveil our hidden potential and expand our possibilities.

The fact is, a child who is Lights On can learn in any learning environment. Their success and flourishing are not dependent on circumstance, or even how the education is delivered. A boring curriculum or less than inspiring teacher does not stop them from achieving. However, a child who is Lights Off can't learn effectively in even the most creative of educational settings. We can tinker all we like with the external learning environment and we might make a difference – to some children. However, equally, we might not move the dial at all. When we shift our focus to strengthening and enhancing a child's internal learning environment, the impact is life-changing.

From anger to feeling invincible

Ruby was nine years old when I started working with her at my creative learning centre. Although it took over a year to turn things around for her and shift her anger, not once did I or her mum give up on her. We could see the brilliance in Ruby. The problem was that Ruby couldn't see it, and this was holding her back. Here are her own words, age eleven:

> 'I definitely had some anger in my body that I had to get out. I didn't want to interact and that was my learning block. When you don't

have that passion, you're trying to find it all the time. As soon as I held a camera in my hand it was like that passion where I don't care about anything else anymore. I wrote an article for the magazine and I wrote at the end "I feel invincible". I'm doing really good at something. No one can take this away from me. It opened all the doors that were padlocked shut because of your anger. It opens different life opportunities. One path you can keep going with your anger and not find that passion and get anywhere. Then there's the other one which is padlocked shut. I'm going to get bolt cutters and I'm going to open those doors. When you find that passion, it changes the whole life-set and you collect all your learning on the way. It's just how far you want to keep on going with it. At that time, I got through so many doors. If this was in schools, people would be astonished at what we can do. It got me through everything. It is definitely a game changer when you find that thing.'

Ruby will always be the child who made me question everything over the first two years of my adventure as an accidental educationalist. She showed me the transformative power of tuning into our Lights On potential as well as the importance of holding that belief for them about their potential to shine. As she stepped into her creatorship, she rose to face challenges in extraordinary ways and really took ownership of her emotional and mental inner world. It was so beautiful to witness her redefine success on her terms and step into who she was born to be.

Let's get the Lights On metric into your family

Your family's relationship with learning changes the moment you normalise being Lights Off as a natural and healthy part of learning. You need both states – Lights On and Lights Off – to flourish. As Betsy's family discovered, 'Lights Off is a messenger, knocking on your door inviting you to grow.' It's so true, so I invite you to have a conversation about what being Lights On and Lights Off means to your family. Here are the first-ever Lights On definitions from an online survey I ran in 2017.

Being Lights On means:

> 'We are mentally and creatively being powered up.'
>
> 'Our mind is flowing with creativity and ideas.'
>
> 'We are motivated to learn, open-minded and like a sponge for absorbing new information.'
>
> 'We are feeling positive and ready to embrace the challenges of the day.'

For three-year-old Aheli, being Lights On feels like 'having rainbows in my heart'. How beautiful is that? Whenever I see a rainbow, I feel a huge sense of awe, wonder and delight. What a powerful feeling to resonate with and tune into for learning.

I want to share another definition, by Jo, that touched my heart when I read it:

> 'I know I am Lights On because I feel light and invincible. The future seems so full of possibilities and excitement. My mind feels clear and I can find the thoughts that I need to move forward. When I see people around me, I feel love towards them and that mirrors back. When faced with challenges, I feel fired up and ready to learn to move forward in this adventure called Life.'

Beautiful.

What does being Lights On and Lights Off mean to you?

If you are feeling nervous about having your initial Lights On conversation with your family, that's normal. Many parents have felt the same and had an immediate Lights Off reaction about taking action. When you claim this adventure is for yourself, too, you just need to invite them to join you. Tune into your fear and blend in some healthy excitement. Imagine what's possible for you all when your lights are fully on, and you have the tools to use being Lights Off to your advantage. Think about your family achieving extraordinary things healthily and sustainably, and notice how you feel if you allow yourself to believe it's possible. Use the question prompts to find out what your family intuitively understands about being Lights On and Lights Off.

What do you think it is like to be learning with your Lights On?

- What are you doing when you feel happy, content, engaged, inspired?
- How does it feel?
- Where do you feel it in your body?
- What thoughts do you have when you are in this Lights On state?
- What is possible for you when you are Lights On?

Also explore what being Lights Off means to you:

- What is it that switches off your lights and makes you feel frustrated, bored, angry or sad?
- Where do you feel it in your body?

YOUR LIGHTS ON AND LIGHTS OFF POTENTIAL

- What thoughts do you have when you are in this Lights Off state?

- What is possible for you when you are Lights Off?

If your family is switched off and disengaged, start by defining Lights Off, as they are more likely to connect with that starting point. You might ask how they feel when learning at school or home. Then ask them how they would like to feel and move towards getting clarity about being Lights On.

Once you've done this, you have officially begun your Lights On Learning adventure. Congratulations!

LIGHTS ON CHECK-IN

Let's use the metric straight away. When you think about having this initial conversation with your family what do you feel? Are you Lights On and raring to go? Or feeling fear that they won't want to get involved? Maybe you are somewhere in the middle? Think about where you are on the Lights On sliding scale below.

Darkness → Dimness → Glimmer → Glow → Brilliance → Radiance
Lights Off   Lights On

1   2   3   4   5   6

Remember, being Lights Off is not a problem, you have an enormous growth opportunity ahead. As you realise that disengagement is a natural and healthy response

LIGHTS ON LEARNING

to feeling disempowered, bored and switched off, I hope you'll understand your family in a new light. In the next chapter, we're going to look at the three core components that are essential if you are to feel safe to shine your brilliance out into the world.

3
Your Lights On Learning Circuitry

My daughter was nine years old when she curled up with our dog one morning and said, 'You may as well send me to prison every day, Mum. That is what it feels like.'

She wasn't being melodramatic, or even angry. It was her tone of resignation and the absence of emotion that concerned me most. My daughter, once happy, inquisitive and hungry to experience life to the full, had dark rings under her eyes. There was no light. No laughter. There appeared to be little hope. This was no longer about her education. It was about safeguarding her mental health.

I felt it as an emotional blow in my gut. A hopelessness that, despite all the work I had done to flex the system and enrich her school life, it wasn't working. She continued to be frustrated by the slow pace. As she described it, 'My learning is fenced in.' Over the years, when I had tried to address how bored she was with her teachers, I felt like a pushy parent.

I was told 'It's not a race, Julia.'

I agree, it is not a race, so why do we even talk about children falling behind? The old-school system puts our children on a conveyor belt that doesn't stop until they come out the other end. It creates fear and confusion in parents, children and teachers as we struggle to make sense of a reality which stifles our growth.

If a child wants to skip, hop and dance their way through their education, we should let them – surely? My daughter wanted to play and explore her curiosity. The standardised assessment system put blinkers on the teachers and brakes on her learning, both of which impacted her mental health. That morning, in what felt like a crisis point, I phoned the school.

'She's not coming back in.'

I deregistered her and elected to home educate, which I acknowledge was a privilege I could afford to do and a legal option here in the UK. People around me thought I was reading too much into it. 'Perhaps it isn't as bad as she is making out. Do you think she's saying what you want to hear because she knows you're listening to Sir Ken Robinson?!'[15] Possibly, but if Sir Ken, the global authority on creativity in education, and my daughter were saying the same thing, I was going to listen!

And listen I did – to more than a thousand children who came through my creative learning centres over the next three years. I discovered that a child's success has far less to do with what happens on the outside than we think. It has much more to do with their internal learning landscape. Over and over again, I saw how a child's true power to learn, grow and achieve came from the thoughts they think, the emotions they feel and the actions they take daily.

Thoughts + Emotions + Action = Outcomes

To keep this front of mind and shine the spotlight upstream of the outcomes, we use the above equation. This focuses our attention on how our inner power is influenced by our thoughts, emotions and actions and makes sure we have three core components connected to the learning process. These are your Heartset, Mindset and Skillset.

---

15 K Robinson, 'Do schools kill creativity?' (2007), www.youtube.com/watch?v=iG9CE55wbtY, accessed 25 August 2024

Your Lights On Learning circuitry

I'd like to invite you to imagine your internal learning circuitry as an interconnected network of circuits that run between your head and heart, and throughout your body. Just as wires transmit electrical signals between the switch and the light in your home, you have networks of neurons that transmit electrical impulses through your brain, heart and nervous system. When your Heartset, Mindset and Skillset are connected and optimised, you have a coherent creative energy flow and your family's potential is limitless. You are plugged in and powered up. How brightly your inner light shines is determined by how these components are activated during the learning process. This determines the choices you make, the actions you take, how you behave and the outcomes you get.

When there is a disconnection, your lights dim or switch off and you feel lost in the dark. Unplugged. Powerless. To quote Carolina, one of the mothers in my community and our resident neuroscientist, 'When you shift your focus to your internal reality you can react in new ways. This is when you can realise your maximum potential. You, and only you, get to decide how you use it, when you use it and whether you use it.'

Let's look at these core components in more detail.

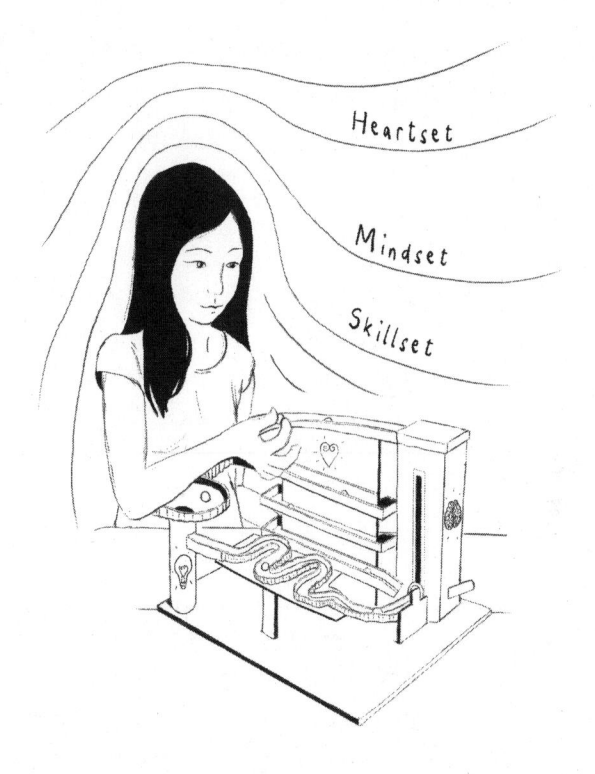

Heartset – your emotional connection

I think of your Heartset as the emotional home to your dreams and desires. It is where you find the courage to explore your curiosities, pursue your passions and commit to a life full of purpose. We've already seen the power of passion to activate your full capacity to learn, create and grow, with Ollie and Ruby. Just as switches control the flow of electricity in your house, your emotions switch on, dim or turn off your lights.

Lights Off emotions, such as fear, anger and sadness, act as the off switch, hindering the flow of energy, creating a loose, glitchy circuit connection and limiting your potential to shine in that moment. These emotions are particularly powerful for growth.

Lights On emotions, such as happiness, hope, joy, love and gratitude are like the on switches. They enable your radiant energy to flow so you can fully explore and express your learning potential.

Accessing your full emotional range

Learning is an emotional experience, and being aware of your inner emotional state transforms your outcomes. In her 'Theory of Constructed Emotions', Lisa Feldman Barret proposes we give meaning to our emotions based on thinking from past experiences and our worldview. This means you are not at the 'mercy of your emotions', instead you get to decide what this 'internal pattern of biological events' means.[16] Butterflies in your tummy can either be experienced as being nervous excitement (Lights On) or anxiety (Lights Off). You choose.

Barret believes, as I have discovered, too, that we 'have the capacity to turn down the dial on emotional suffering' and 'curate our unique life experience'. When

---

16 L Feldman, *How Emotions Are Made: The secret life of the brain* (Mariner Books, 2018)

we develop our self-awareness of our internal state, known as interoception, we can use our emotions as subtle signals to direct our attention and focus. We can take decisive action to open up our field of potentiality. It's magical to see.

The Lights On metric builds the habit of noticing a shift from Lights On to Lights Off so you can use your breath, quieten your mind or go outside and move physically to calibrate back to being Lights On. The metric also enables you to determine the difference between healthy disengagement that you can harness for growth, or become aware of a persistent underlying cause or health concern you need to address with the support of medical or mental health professionals.

Your heart ensures you flourish

Obviously, we're all aware of the important role our hearts play in keeping us physically alive. However, our hearts also play a vital role in helping us flourish and feel mentally and spiritually alive. Research by the HeartMath Institute shows that two-way communication between our heart and brain enables us to create heart-brain coherence and balance the sympathetic and parasympathetic nervous systems.[17] Dr J Andrew Armour, a pioneering neurocardiologist,

---

17 HeartMath Institute, 'What is heart coherence?' (13 September 2022), www.heartmath.com/blog/health-and-wellness/what-is-heart-coherence/, accessed 25 August 2024

also discovered our hearts have an intricate network of 40,000 neurons, which he referred to as the heart-brain.[18]

From a scientific, intuitive or educational standpoint, then, it doesn't make sense to leave your family's hearts out of your education strategy. Bringing passion, purpose and play into learning is the most powerful way to energise and supercharge their engagement. Quite simply, Lights On Learning feels so good and is great for your mental, emotional and physical health.

Your emotional connection turns consumers into creators

Take a moment to think about whether you have a family who embraces their innate gifts, strengths and superpowers to move from good to great and own their individuality. Do they express their authentic spirit as inspiring creators, using their passions to build their mental and emotional resilience? Or have they disconnected from their natural-born gifts and stayed stuck as passive consumers of other people's or, increasingly, AI's, creations?

---

18 HeartMath Institute, 'The "little brain in the heart"' (no date), www.heartmath.org/our-heart-brain/, accessed 25 August 2024

Mindset – the mental connection

Your brain is of course central to your Lights On Learning circuitry and acts as a command centre. It sends information through an extensive interconnected network of between 80–128 billion neurons within your nervous system.[19] Just as wires transmit electrical signals between the exchange and your home, your neurons communicate throughout your nervous system via electrical impulses and chemical messengers, known as neurotransmitters, such as dopamine, oxytocin, serotonin and endorphins.

Your thoughts, like resistors in an electrical circuit, regulate your emotions and nervous system. They sharpen your focus and attention, affecting how you express yourself. In a very real way, your thoughts define the edges of your comfort zone and the boundaries of your limitations. They can either hold you back or set you free to express your potential.

Lights Off thoughts – 'I can't do this, it's too hard. I'm rubbish and probably going to fail anyway, so why bother?' – cause you to shrink, hide and play it safe.

Lights On thoughts – 'I can do this. I have what it takes. I can do hard things' – will provide you with a sense of expansion where anything feels possible.

---

19   L Feldman, *Seven and a Half Lessons About the Brain* (Picador, 2021)

We have a lot of Lights Off thoughts

The challenge comes because of the sheer number of thoughts we have each day. Only a small percentage of our thoughts need our conscious mind. Most of our thinking comes from automated programmes hard-wired in our unconscious mind during our formative childhood experiences within our homes, schools and communities. Our neurocircuitry, as parents, caregivers or educators, impacts our child's emotions, motor skills, behavioural control, logic, language and memory, more than we might like to admit.[20] This is why Lights On Learning is about whole-family transformation, and not just for your child who is disengaged. Imagine using the power of rewiring your Lights Off circuitry to change the generational legacy for future generations to come.

A family of 'cans' versus the 'cannots' is dependent on your mental connection

Take a moment to reflect on whether your child believes they 'can' find a way to figure it out when things get challenging, regardless of how long it might take, or if they become stuck telling themselves they 'can't', and give up when things don't fall into place easily for them.

---

20 Center on the Developing Child, 'Brain architecture' (Harvard University, 2015), https://developingchild.harvard.edu/science/key-concepts/brain-architecture/, accessed 25 August 2024

Dr Carol Dweck's research on mindset clearly shows that what we believe to be true about ourselves as learners matters.[21] Our thoughts and beliefs impact our motivation, performance and achievement. With a growth mindset, we see learning as a process and value mistakes as part of success. We understand that we can use our brain's neuroplasticity to grow. What once was impossible, like walking for a toddler, becomes possible when we train our brains to create neural networks that work for us.

In contrast, when we have a fixed mindset, we are more reactive as we view intelligence as something we either have or don't have. This leads to fear of failure. We give up easily, procrastinate or avoid the task completely. We obsess about the outcome and miss being present in the process. I saw this a lot in the high achievers I worked with in schools. They wanted the external validation of grades as affirmation that they were doing it right, as so often their parents did, too. They certainly did not want to appear to get anything wrong. Tell them what to do and they will do it. Give them an open-ended problem to solve, or ask them to do a second draft, and they would resist and, at times, crumble.

---

21 C Dweck, *Mindset: Changing the way you think to fulfill your potential* (Robinson, 2017)

Skillset – the physical connection

Lights On Learning brings your heart, head and hands into the process of learning, making it an active, physical and fully embodied experience. As your child develops the practical skills and capabilities linked to their 'switch' (the creative expression that lights them up), they start turning their dreams, desires and ideas into tangible, physical reality. Now you can invest time, energy and resources to develop the relevant skills that enable them to pursue their big, bold dreams with courage.

Think about a toddler learning to walk. To start with, they have no neural network to put one foot in front of the other in a coordinated way. To develop that skill, they must practise, fall, get back up and try again. During this learning phase, neurons 'fire and wire together'[22] into a neural network that makes it possible to take their first wobbly steps. Their persistence, repetition and commitment to the outcome strengthen the synaptic connections (the microscopic gap between neurons) and speed up communication within the neural network. This is ultimately what learning is: the wiring of highly efficient automated neural circuits that can lead to mastery.

---

22 C Keysers and V Gazzola, 'Hebbian learning and predictive mirror neurons for actions, sensations and emotions', *Philosophical Transactions of the Royal Society B: Biological Sciences*, 369/1644 (2014), doi:https://doi.org/10.1098/rstb.2013.0175

Your Skillset gifts you a collaborative advantage over a competitive advantage

Think about whether your child has real, authentic, tangible evidence of their learning and growth potential that makes them stand out from the crowd, or are they still competing purely with old-school metrics and extra-curricular activities that millions of others around the world also have? It is their emotional, mental and physical connection to learning that will give them the edge and lead to their success. When all three are working in harmony, you have a coherent energy flow and your inner light shines brightly. Lights On. This is when you feel a deep sense of meaning and fulfilment. If one component is dialled down, or disconnected, your lights may stay on but not as brightly. When you face a significant challenge or are triggered in some way, your lights might go off altogether. Becoming more aware of your internal state is key to building your family's mental, emotional and physical resilience.

The gift of your brain's neuroplasticity

According to Michael Merzenich, 'Your brain – every brain – is a work in progress. It is "plastic". From the day we're born to the day we die, it continuously revises and remodels, improving or slowly declining, as a function of how we use it.'[23]

---

[23] M Merzenich, *How You Can Make Your Brain Smarter Every Day* (Forbes, 2013), www.forbes.com/sites/nextavenue/2013/08/06/how-you-can-make-your-brain-smarter-every-day/, accessed 25 August 2024

Your brain's ability to continually reorganise and form new neural connections is known as 'neuroplasticity'. In the example of a toddler learning to walk, their brain's structure changes to support the expression of this new skill. These neural pathways become more efficient the more they're used, and can also be pruned away if you stop using them. This is why Lights On Learning builds in time for exploration, problem-solving, critical thinking and learning new skills to stimulate your brain's capacity to adapt and grow throughout your life.

I've seen the rapid skill development and cognitive growth that happens when the Lights On Learning circuitry is lit up. When children start to see evidence of what they can achieve they become unstoppable.

From underperforming to inspired and motivated in less than eight hours

Take six-year-old Oscar, for example. He was underachieving at school, and not putting in the effort. His teacher described him as 'lazy' and capable of so much more. Our job was to supplement his school learning to help him discover and switch on his brilliance. Here's how we used the three core components of his Lights On Learning circuitry to transform him as a learner. Over four sessions, Liz, one of my creative learning designers, and our young maths intern, Louis, worked with Oscar in our Makery.

Step one: switch on his Heartset. What did he love to do? He loved to draw houses. His father was an architect, so no real surprise there.

Step two: grow his Mindset. Where were his edges? What intentional activity would help him see what he could achieve beyond his comfort zone? We chose to use a process of draft critique, as developed by Ron Berger, as our growth tool.[24]

Step three: activate his Skillset. What skills does he need to fully express his passions? In this case, we chose technical drawing of an impossible triangle to align with his Heartset.

Step four: give him time. We gave him some dedicated time during our two-hour after-school sessions for him to focus on this activity.

When Oscar came to show me his final draft I was blown away. He was so incredibly proud. Just look at how visible his growth is:

---

24   R Berger, *An Ethic of Excellence* (Heinemann Educational Books, 2003)

Step five: celebrate and reflect. Our hearts and brains love celebrating, so reflective conversations to super-size micro-wins ensure growth is fully integrated and 'hardwired' in for future success.

Step six: future cast. A simple projection of what is possible from this point forward activates the Heartset to dream even bigger and leads the Mindset and Skillset to follow.

Oscar was excited to share his newfound wisdom, and the storyteller in me wanted to capture this pivotal moment so we made a short film together:

> 'Nothing is impossible if you keep on trying over and over again… I get really frustrated when I get it wrong but I still keep on trying… As I did more and more of this draft two, I got more confident and more confident… On my draft four, I was, like, it doesn't look quite right. So I tried again… I feel really amazed and proud of myself.'[25]

Lights On Learning changed the way Oscar viewed himself as a learner, in such a great way, and of course, the transformation was seen back in the home and classroom, too. What more do we want for our children but to feel great about who they are and what

---

25 Lights On, 'How the impossible triangle changed the life of Oscar' (2016), www.youtube.com/watch?v=avH3TiVhtJc, accessed 25 August 2024

they are capable of achieving? Just like Ollie, Esme, Seb and Ruby, Oscar felt a huge sense of self-belief and confidence in who he was. This changed his attitude in school and at home.

Oscar's achievement was pivotal for us as a team. The impossible triangle exercise became one of our 'Wired For Learning' activities we did with every school group that visited. It was phenomenal to see the insights they gained about themselves as they shifted as learners, from something being impossible to possible. From 'I can't' to 'I can'. From Lights Off to Lights On.

If Oscar had stopped at draft one, what would he have learned about himself? 'Well done, Oscar. Great try.' He was only six, after all, so what could we expect? If we set a culture of learning that stops at the first draft, we limit our children's potential with our low expectations. By guiding Oscar to aim high and believe in himself, he expressed his potential in ways that transformed him as a learner, in and out of school. In less than eight hours!

Learning is iterative and comes alive when your heart intuitively leads the way and energises your emotional drive. It will always dream bigger than your head or hands are ready for, and it makes you courageously vulnerable enough to play with both love and fear together. As you open up to curiosity and tune into awe and wonder, you can shift into what feels like a more expansive, safe space to take action. As you activate your Heartset, you naturally grow your Mindset and develop your relevant Skillset. It's all part of becoming a Lights On learner who loves and lives to learn. However, your Heartset on its own leaves you vulnerable to dreaming; it is the combination of all three components that brings so much richness for learning, discovery, growth and mastery. Learning in this way can quite literally last a lifetime!

LIGHTS ON CHECK-IN

In the next chapter, we're going to use my simple activity that will help you find your family's 'switches', but first, use these question prompts to reflect on your family of learners.

Are all three components connected, allowing you and your family to shine bright?

If not, which one is not fully engaged? Their Heartset, Mindset or Skillset? All of them?

Which ones are loosely wired, giving you inconsistent results and flickering lights?

4
Flicking The Switch

Imagine for a moment you are a nine-year-old artist and storyteller, born to create characters, conjure up worlds and craft stories. It is so strong in your Heartset that you can't ignore it. Every day you look around you and find inspiration. In the trees you see characters come alive, which you yearn to draw, paint and bring to life. Your heart lights up your learning circuitry, and your mind is so expansive there are no limits. Your creative energy is ready to flow with ease and create a video-game series that rivals Pokémon. You can see it all – the sprites, the easter eggs, the game lore, everything. It is so clear and even more real than the video games you love to play.

As you immerse yourself in your imaginary world, people around you think you're daydreaming. Not focusing or paying attention. They worry you're falling behind, but really you are in creation mode, homing in on all the small details that, for now, only you can see. You want to get it all out onto paper, animated on a screen, coded within a video game, but when? Suppressing your desire to create for the six hours a day, five days a week, 39 weeks of the year that you spend in school becomes too much. Even at home, it all stays in your head. Unexpressed. No one understands the magic you have bubbling inside and it is exhausting containing it within you. You feel like you are going to explode and become drained. Depleted. Exhausted. Lights Off.

Everyone around you seems concerned. 'What is wrong with you?' But you don't know.

Imagine being that nine-year-old – how would it feel?

'Dead inside', is how nine-year-old Max, the creator I've described above, told me. It's heartbreaking to hear such a young boy, with so much to offer the world, having his creative spirit crushed. Without the mental, emotional and energetic charge of exploring and expressing what he loved to do, Max started refusing school. Quite simply, as you can imagine, it did not feel like a good place to be.

I first met Kayte when she joined my online programme to help her son, Max. It was clear straight away that he was born to draw, create characters and craft stories.

As Kayte made space for him to do so, his lights came back on. She began to learn to lead him to use his artistic and storytelling 'switch' to supercharge his learning. As she began to let go of her own old-school thinking and develop her leadership skills, he began to create characters, stories and whole new worlds. He moved from pencil and paper to digital art, using software tools like Procreate and Blender. He took his ideas to a new level and developed a concept for a multimedia game called 'Soul Monsters', for which he built a website. All this tangible evidence of his Heartset, Mindset and Skillset working in alignment activated his Lights On state and made him feel great.

When I interviewed Max and asked how he felt now he was creating, he said, 'Amazing!'

From feeling dead inside – Lights Off – to feeling amazing – Lights On.

This all happened quickly once his mum increased his engagement through his passions, enabling him to be open to re-engaging in traditional subjects like English and maths – as we saw with Ollie, Ruby and Oscar.

Your Heartset is always ready

For some children, like Max and Ollie, that innate desire to express themselves is so powerful that it stays at the forefront of their hearts and minds. They can't stop thinking about it, which disrupts their academic learning. These are the children who respond really well to Lights On Learning, giving them the time to bring their Heartset, Mindset and Skillset into play. It's an immediate effect. A flick of a switch from Lights Off to Lights On. Now nothing can extinguish the light that shines within them. Often these children are neurodiverse or have a high entry level to their natural gift. Allow them to shine, and their focus, attention and achievement improve.

For other children, their desire to creatively express themselves can get buried just below the surface. Maybe it is no longer being nurtured, fully recognised or valued, so its light dims over time but hasn't fully gone out. These children are often the high performers who begin to realise that their academic success is prized over their creative explorations. They also respond well to Lights On Learning but often need more support to strengthen their Mindset and trust they are safe to explore, experiment and not be perfect.

Some children's Heartset has never had the chance to spark. With no opportunity to experience the pure joy that comes with having a passion burning bright inside, they can feel perpetually Lights Off. They have little evidence of, or belief in, their potential for greatness. I feel Lights On Learning is essential for these children. It helps them build up their reserves of mental, emotional and physical resilience to overcome the everyday challenges they face from living largely in survival mode.

My team and I have worked with children, young people and adults who have been in all these scenarios. Whatever a child's situation, and no matter how strong their protective armour is, I've found their heart is waiting patiently for them to have the opportunity, and courage, to express it. Regardless of how long their Heartset has been disconnected, they were able to reconnect and express it again. Surprisingly fast.

I worked with one teenager who had no idea what they loved to do. They were struggling in school, truanting and getting into trouble. I gave them an iPad to take photos with, as a simple way for me to understand how they saw the world. Wow! Every photo was a close-up of tiny details that most of us would never see. Where I might look at the big picture, they zoomed in and saw beautiful patterns and shapes. I asked them if they had noticed this about themselves. They hadn't. I gave them access to fabric, a sewing machine and a creative brief to make something. I wanted to see how this might be expressed in a different medium. Again, wow! They created an intricate, neat, beautiful fabric collage, again with attention to tiny details. Just like their photography, their work was captivating to look at.

Unfortunately, I didn't get to continue working with them, but I will always remember that even in someone who had no idea of their natural brilliance and had never been given the chance to express it, there was their gift, waiting to be witnessed by someone who believed they, like everyone else, had something unique and beautiful inside that they were born to express.

Regardless of their life experiences and circumstances, children need time for passion-led projects to flourish. They also need at least one adult in their life who knows how to help them find that 'thing that switches on their lights', and who will give them space and time to explore it. Ideally, that person is you – their parent. When a child becomes ambitious about what they can do, they willingly jump the hurdles they need to open up the next level of their game. They become happier, more fulfilled and unstoppable, constantly expanding their Mindset and Skillset to unlock the grander vision within their Heartset. The act of stepping outside of their comfort zone energises, motivates and leads them into that state of optimal learning. What they can achieve today is not their limit. They understand that becoming great at what they love to do requires persistence, practice and patience.

Flicking on your family's switches

Over the three years that I ran my creative learning centre, Explorium, I learned alongside children, aged four right up to their early twenties. Early on, I noticed that, when given the freedom to learn, they self-organised to play to their strengths and express themselves in a Lights On way. They would head straight to the Lego box, for example. Or grab an iPad and begin creating digitally. Maybe they'd go to the dressing-up rail and begin to create characters and craft stories. I therefore named this their 'switch' as it lit them up faster than anything else and made them more mentally and emotionally resilient to challenges.

Here are a few of the most common Lights On power switches I noticed, but this is by no means an exhaustive list.

Digital wizards are happiest when creating and exploring with technology, and they like learning on the fly. They are comfortable solving problems through trial and error. I discovered my son's digital wizardry switch at age seven.

Wordsmiths are always conjuring up and sharing stories and being playful with words, and they are often engaged in imaginative play. My daughter is a wordsmith, something I discovered when she was age six.

Tinkerers, engineers or makers are hands-on kids, always making and creating something physical using

Lego, plasticine, cardboard, wood, metal or recycled bits and bobs. They are often conceptual thinkers, visualising their ideas in 3D, and are natural solution seekers who love overcoming obstacles.

Artists bring visual ideas to life through their creative expression such as drawings, paintings, collages, dance, theatre or music. They likely have their unique style emerging at a young age.

Movers love the freedom that being physical gives them, having space to move around and being hands-on and active in the learning experience. This is a great switch for working on Mindset and Skillset because they know that to become great at any sport or physical activity requires practice, patience and persistence. In fact, one of my seventeen-year-old interns, Matt, was a skateboarder. We used this to his advantage to learn and grow exponentially. After seven years of working together, he left to set up his own business. Within three years he had a seven-figure business! So bring on the skater mindset, I say!

There are also the performers, scientists, mathematicians, dancers, chefs, entrepreneurs, musicians and many more. Don't get too hung up on it, the key is to observe how your child, or yourself, chooses to bring ideas into tangible, physical form. Don't worry about pigeon-holing them, this is merely the entry point where they are likely to be naturally more courageous and open to exploring and creating. From this starting point, they will naturally extend outwards into other areas you never expected. They will develop a wide variety of skills and use an interdisciplinary approach to problem solving.

It's incredible to see what a child, young person or adult can achieve when learning through their switches and tuning into their Lights On creatorship. It highlights how much potential is being wasted in our old-school consumption model, where passions and purpose are left on the sidelines. When we try to grow our children's Mindsets without first engaging the Heartset, it will feel like heavy lifting. You'll find yourself talking at them, but without conviction, because you don't fully believe what you are saying. Unless you walk this walk, it's like telling them to 'just put on the lights so you can see' but they are lost in the darkness, thinking, 'I can't; I don't know where the switch is and I'm scared of what I might see if I do.' Inside, you are also thinking, 'I don't know either.' Therefore, heart first, always, and then engage the head, for you and your family, and you'll start to see some extraordinary learning begin to happen as they take full ownership of their ability to shine.

Lights On learners are phenomenal! If finding their switch is your starting point to unlock their potential, I suggest you do it. In fact, let's meet James and his incredible mum, Lisa, to encourage you.

From rock bottom to award-winning young entrepreneur in less than a year

When Lisa came to me, her twelve-year-old son, James, was struggling academically and his mental health was at rock bottom. She was feeling helpless and desperate for a solution as her son was failing in school and had lost all self-belief. As Lisa moved away from being a victim of an outdated system and stepped into a leadership role, everything changed in such a short space of time.

It was clear that James' lights were off at school and this was impacting his mental health and his ability to learn. It was also clear that James had a passion, was a natural entrepreneur and wanted to learn. As Lisa brought his entrepreneurial switch centre-stage and focused on what James was naturally good at, she brought his Heartset, Mindset and Skillset into the dynamic. Lisa saw how hungry he was to learn and, despite the challenges she would face as a single mum, chose to home-educate him. On his thirteenth birthday, she announced he would never have to spend another day in school. Lights On!

In just nine months, Lisa transformed her son from disengaged to highly engaged. As James explored his entrepreneurial 'switch', he became an award-winning, celebrity-endorsed young entrepreneur. He appeared on local and national media and raised over £1K for his local children's hospital through his social enterprise project. Now that's what I call activated Lights On potential!

By listening to her heart and being courageous enough to take action, Lisa gifted her son the opportunity to explore what he loved and was naturally good at. In doing so, she reignited her passion for learning, wrote and published a children's book, and started her own side business as a life coach. This is what is possible when you bring Lights On Learning into your home: your whole family transforms. Because it begins with you, whether you are ready to admit that or not.

What is it that switches on your family's lights?

What Lisa achieved is possible for you. Just because the professionals are failing to light up your child's love of learning, it doesn't mean you will. With some simple changes, you can, as a family of Lights On learners, achieve so much. In fact, as Ruby said, you'll be astonished by what you can all do.

Ready?

Step one: Ask a simple question

To build on your conversations from Chapter 1 about being Lights On and Off, you want to ask your child the following question:

If you could wake up every morning and do the thing you love the most, what would it be?

Finding out if they know the answer to this is the crucial first step. I am a big fan of brainstorms. A big sheet of paper and lots of colourful pens! You can learn a lot about a child from how they approach it. Some fill up the page with colour, drawings and words and are clear, and others may be a bit more reticent or say they don't know.

Now, if they say 'playing video games, watching YouTube videos or being on social media', don't dismiss it. Note it down and then ask 'What else?' What do they love doing when they are creating rather than playing someone else's creation? If they were to design a video game themselves, like Max, which part would they like most? Coding, strategy, drawing, designing the levels? I've run a few video-game projects with groups of children and they always self-select the part they want to contribute based on their switch.[26]

---

26 Lights On, '"The Box" – A game design concept project' (2016), www.youtube.com/watch?v=csDkWU74hQM, accessed 25 August 2024

Step two: Hold a simple activity

Set up a learning carousel – a sweet shop of creative goodies for you all to explore! A pick-and-mix of tinkering stations that offers choice, autonomy and ownership over what they explore, how they play and use their imagination. Lay different activities out in a room, your garden or throughout your whole house. You might want to include some Lego, paints, an animation station, cardboard and some maker tools, old technology to take apart, a sewing machine and dressing-up clothes. You don't need all these resources, so if you are limited in what you have, or by space, then start small with one thing you know they like doing and one that might be a new exploration. Make your learning carousel your own, based on what you have available. Then jump in and explore alongside them, making the most of this time to create through your own switch or reconnect with it after all these years!

Step three: Collect some simple data

Give yourself at least an hour and be curious about what they choose to do. How they interact with the different opportunities tells you a lot about who they are as a learner. Make a mental note of which tinkering station you noticed where they were most Lights On. As they move around the carousel, think about these questions:

- Are they excited and highly inquisitive, or do they not know where to even begin?
- Do they head straight to one station and spend all their time there, or do they explore every station but not settle?
- Do they create digitally or physically?

Watch out for their energy levels and notice when they move between being Lights On and Lights Off. If a child needs a lot of your time or involvement, simply note when it is they ask for help. Is it when they get stuck? Is it to ask for ideas in the first place? Or is it because they are hungry and don't want to stop what they are doing but need a snack?!

The key is to be open and nonjudgemental about how your child interacts and engages with the carousel, and, of course, how you feel exploring, too.

Throw a learning carousel party!

If you have young children, it can be a fun idea to do a learning carousel with a small group of their friends. This will create a healthy buzz in the room, as they all get stuck into the station that interests them the most or start collaborating.

We've done learning carousels with children aged four to eighteen (in fact, even with adults), and they just work. If you are thinking, 'I've got teenagers, they are just going to roll their eyes,' then this is likely to be a lack of confidence about your ability to enrol and lead them on this creative adventure. Get in there with them to role model your own Lights On creative energy and use this as a great opportunity to explore and create yourself. On one of my birthdays, my teenagers threw a learning carousel party for me, which I loved.

If your child has been Lights Off for a while, you might want to put out one thing at a time to avoid it feeling overwhelming. Be assured though, I've worked with lots of children who don't know what they love to do at first, and it is usually a contributing reason for their disengagement. Find their switch and you'll see them light up.

A new learning adventure opens up

Once you know your child's switch, it changes everything and opens up the door to increased engagement and unprecedented growth. As you discover your family's switches, curiosities and unique sense of wonder, you'll ignite a passion for learning within you all. You will fall in love with being you and feel awe at what you can achieve using your natural gifts, talents and strengths. Sound good?

So, from now on, never dismiss the power of the switch. It is simple and highly effective, and it's impossible to build an effective learning strategy without it. When you bring your child's switch centre-stage of their learning, it changes everything. Leading your child to be an engaged, inspired, creative, self-led learner becomes relatively straightforward from this point on.

Heartset + Mindset + Skillset = Fully expressed!

Let's recap what it means to be Lights On and Lights Off before we dive a layer deeper in Part Two:

- Being Lights On and Lights Off refers to the internal state of being, based on what you are feeling and thinking at any given moment.

- Your internal mental, emotional and physical state of being affects the choices you make, the actions you take and the results you get in life.

- When you are Lights On, you are in creation mode and open to the limitless field of possibilities around you.

- When you are Lights Off, you are stuck in survival mode until you harness the incredible power within this state and transform it into a growth opportunity.

- Someone who is Lights On can access even the most traditional ways of learning and find joy in their education.

- Someone who is Lights Off, and who doesn't know how to use this state for growth, can't even access what is on offer in the most creative learning environment.

LIGHTS ON CHECK-IN

You've got your family's definition of what it means to be Lights On and Lights Off. Now, over the next day or two, intentionally look for at least three times when you see their natural brilliance shine through. When you see it in their eyes, it's like their lights have come on.

Make a note in your journal of:

- What they look like when their lights are on
- What they were doing
- How it makes you feel
- What thoughts you have
- Where you feel it in your body

Anchor this in as a memory you feel in your heart when you notice your child naturally lit up.

In Part Two, we're going to explore the nuances of your Lights On and Lights Off states, because now you've found your family's switch, you've got a whole light spectrum to explore!

PART TWO
GETTING WIRED FOR LEARNING

5
The Lights On Spectrum

I've always had a strong sense of justice. I remember being about seven years old when a group of children surrounded a boy in the school playground. They were laughing at him, saying he liked to play with dolls. I walked into the group and told them to back off. I can't recall exactly what I said, or how everyone reacted, but I do know they stopped, and it never happened again. I feel proud when I think of my younger self instinctively having the courage to speak out for something I knew was wrong.

This changemaker spirit in me has guided me throughout my life as a filmmaker, educationalist, writer and entrepreneur. Most importantly, though, it has also been my inner compass as a mother. When it became clear that school was not going to be smooth sailing for my daughter, I became a parent governor. I figured that if Esme felt stifled, unhappy and unfulfilled at age four, then other children probably did, too.

As I began my research into education, Sir Ken Robinson and his famous Ted Talk, 'Do Schools Kill Creativity?'[27] was, of course, my starting point. I quickly discovered Professor Guy Claxton from the Centre of Real World Learning,[28] and Richard Gerver's pioneering work at the Grange Primary School.[29] They were my early introduction to how education can be when teachers, schools and communities collaborate.

I 'found' myself chair of the PTA, which, as a social introvert, wasn't a natural role for me, but I became excited by a vision. Imagine if we, as a group of parents, could contribute enrichment opportunities through our talents, skills and our passion for our children to love being at school. That's exactly what we did. We won the National Parent and Teacher Association's (NCPTA) Gold Star Award for 'Changing the Life of the School' in 2010. The lead-up to this recognition was joining creative forces with two other parents, Emmaline and Liz, and mobilising the whole school community. We ran a highly ambitious and impactful project: a big top circus

---

27 K Robinson, 'Do schools kill creativity?' (2007), www.youtube.com/watch?v=iG9CE55wbtY, accessed 25 August 2024
28 G Claxton, *What's the Point of School? Rediscovering the heart of education* (Oneworld, Imp, 2013)
29 R Gerver, *Creating Tomorrow's Schools Today: Education – our children – their futures* (Continuum, 2010)

starring all 106 pupils at the school. We performed two ninety-minute shows to over 600 spectators. It was magical. We had kids on motorbikes, horses, trapezes and silks. We had clowns, jugglers, hula hoopers and performance poets.

So many parents used passions, talents and skills they hadn't expressed in years. It was an incredible achievement for such a tiny, rural village school. We came together and achieved something truly extraordinary, creating inner-smile memories that would last a lifetime. It was a life-defining moment for many of us. Unforgettable. When given the vision and opportunity to do so, we, as a community, chose to shine. The work we did together as parents over the next couple of years changed my life forever.

Immersed in radiance

I remember sitting backstage, celebrating and feeling totally in awe of what we had achieved. I could feel this energy buzzing throughout my body. It was as if I had connected with what I was here to do. This was something I'd been asking myself since I was nine years old: 'Why am I here? What am I here to do?'

I remember asking my dad, who was on such a clear mission, 'How do I find my thing?'

He replied, 'You'll find it.'

It was frustrating at the time. I wanted a roadmap. I wanted to be shown the way. In fact, looking back now, I probably wanted it to be handed to me on a plate. However, what I felt in him was trust. Trust in me that I would discover my bigger purpose.

And there I was. Forty years old, wearing false eyelashes, a pink wig and a corset, experiencing this heartfelt sense of awe. I saw infinite possibilities unfolding if I was courageous enough to show up as my truest self and lead people to express their brilliance. I was here to help others shine their inner light out into the world, for them to step into living the life they were born to live. As we wrapped up the circus, I returned home full of excitement and radiance, the energy of success still resonating through me.

Cascading to darkness

Within the hour, I was in hospital with my three-year-old son. He was having an asthma attack and the emergency doctor was cross with me. 'He is really quite ill, you know?' I felt judged as a mother. I remember a strange mix of emotions. On the one hand, I was still experiencing some of the neurochemical high of my achievement, but here I was cascaded into darkness, full of fear for my son's life.

Up on the ward, the nurse filling in her form asked for my occupation. I felt confused. What did I do? No longer really a filmmaker. Was I a circus director now?! I began to tell her about the circus and she cut me off.

'So you are a mum?'

Just like that, my bubble of self-awe burst.

Despite the huge success I was feeling, in reality, I wasn't strong on who I was anymore. I guess I was 'just' a mum. A bad one. Having grown up believing my generation of women could have it all, my career sabbatical from being a BAFTA and Grierson nominated documentary maker to 'stay-at-home' mum wasn't an easy transition. My mother was an excellent role model. Always there for me and my sister. A strong presence. Rock solid. She worked from home, supporting my father to grow their international charity. I always knew, if and when I needed her, she would be there. I wanted my children to feel that about me: that they were my top priority. Yet I still had this yearning to do more, be more and to fulfil why I was here.

The circus empowered me to step into the identity of a mum with a changemaker spirit. It gave me my first real taste of how I could use my children's journey through education and my natural-born strengths to co-create with others and keep parents engaged with their children's learning. I was hungry for more, and no one was going to take that away from me.

Since then, I've been relentless in my pursuit of understanding how to harness our human potential to achieve extraordinary things together. We are systematically dimming our children's lights and keeping them stumbling around in the dark by asking them to leave their potential for greatness outside the school gates. Lights On Learning makes it impossible for your family to hide their radiance from the world because you know how to lead them out of the dark and activate their full light spectrum.

Your family's Lights On spectrum

Your family's ability to shine and flourish is nuanced. Think of it as having a dial or dimmer switch to calibrate the exact luminosity you want at any given moment. Do you want dark and moody? Is it a warm, contented glow you are after? Or does this moment require your brilliance to light up the room? You get to choose.

As Katrin, a home-educating mother of three, shared: 'I realise it is less about being Lights On or Off, and more about having the awareness of which state I am currently in.' Awareness of your inner state of being is key. Just as an electrician diagnoses where the circuit in your house has blown, you can become a sparky within your family, fine-tuning your inner mental and emotional state to give stability, balance and increased capacity. Understanding that your mental, emotional and physical connection to learning is fluid and dynamic gives you flexibility and ownership over what you can achieve. While you can be totally Lights On, feeling the full neurochemical high of love, joy and gratitude, you can also quickly flip to Lights Off. Like my circus-to-hospital experience. This can feel like you are on an emotional rollercoaster. Invincible one moment and then hugely vulnerable and scared the next. It is a volatile emotional and mental pattern until you know how to stabilise it and use the nuances to your advantage.

I want to thank the small group of mothers who were the first to track their families' Lights On and Lights Off status with me three times a day. It was clear that the binary metric was restrictive. Recording being Lights Off every day was disheartening and kept us in a negative frame of mind. Equally, recording being Lights On all the time felt disingenuous. Were we really Lights On all the time? No, of course not. As Sarah, a yoga teacher and mother of two, insightfully reflected:

> 'I've started to see that Lights On and Lights Off are two ends of a spectrum. Neither is better than the other. Travelling between the two is where the real creativity of our lives is expressed. That's why we feel stuck if we hang out for too long in one or the other without the surrender and letting go required to move into the opposite state. We must travel with trust between Lights On and Lights Off, guided by our hearts, to feel truly alive.'

LIGHTS ON LEARNING

It felt natural to have six levels – three Lights Off and three Lights On. I combined the group's insights, reflections and data, along with the wisdom I have gained as a neurocoach to over a hundred parents. I then created a reference guide to bring definition and clarity to the mental and emotional patterns within the six signatures: Darkness, Dimness, Glimmer, Glow, Brilliance and Radiance.[30]

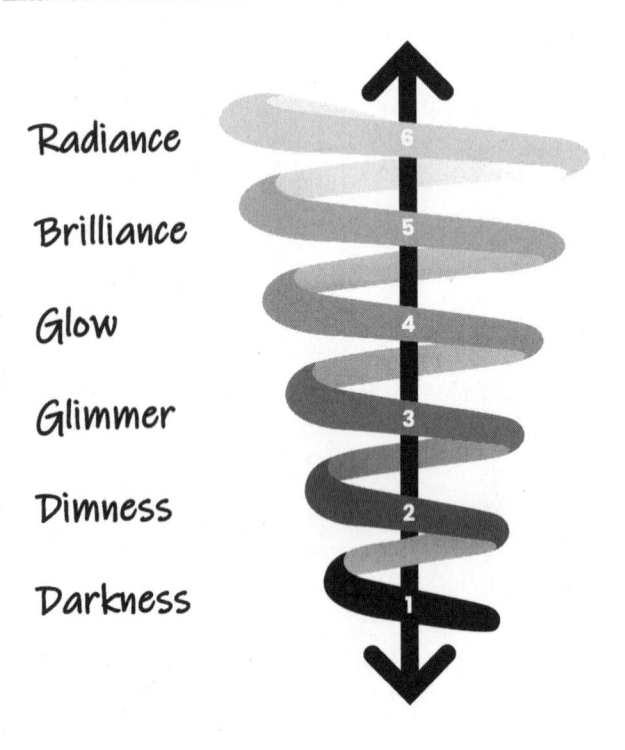

Radiance — 6
Brilliance — 5
Glow — 4
Glimmer — 3
Dimness — 2
Darkness — 1

---

30 There were three main sources I used to understand a hierarchy of emotions: B Brown, *Atlas of the Heart* (Random House, 2021); DR Hawkins, *Letting Go: The pathway of surrender* (Hay House, Inc, 2018); BD Schneider, *Energy Leadership: Transforming your workplace and your life from the core* (J Wiley & Sons, Inc, 2008)

The essence of each signature

Your Lights On spectrum will be unique to you. When you become aware of the subtle nuances and shifts in your mental and emotional state, and how they feel within your body, you will have your Lights On and Lights Off blueprint. You can use this to calibrate your learning circuitry (emotional, mental and physical connection) by shifting energetically from Lights Off to Lights On and rewiring the Lights Off neural circuits. It's like upgrading the electrical blueprint in your house. I grew up in a fifteenth-century house, so I know all about dodgy wiring and frequent power cuts! I've also gone deep into my own neurocircuitry and so everything I share about these Lights On and Lights Off signatures I also know from personal experience to be my truth. Before we do the internal rewiring job, we need to get clarity on what the different signatures feel like.

A cautionary note

We start with Darkness and ascend to Radiance, so you move energetically from Lights Off to Lights On. Even reading about the Lights Off signatures may cause you to feel agitated or panicky. If you have any unresolved trauma, consider doing this next step with a trusted family member, friend, coach or therapist, or have them on standby for support. If you are currently in a very Lights Off place, I suggest you skip ahead and start at Glimmer, and come back to

Darkness and Dimness when you feel psychologically safe to do so. Trust yourself on this. However, if you do start with Darkness, please also know that, as you read through to Radiance, your thoughts and emotions will shift, too. My advice is, therefore, to keep reading and notice your energetic shift as it happens in real-time.

Having said this, when you have this in-depth insight into why you are showing up in your life, as you are, it is life-changing. This is a point of no return. Are you ready?

1. Darkness: Disconnected energy – exhausted

Being in Darkness feels like wading through treacle or trying to look through a heavy fog. There's a pervasive sense of hopelessness and apathy. Your emotional, mental and physical energy is at its lowest. It is difficult to find motivation and every task feels too big. For me, in the early years of motherhood, even the washing up sometimes felt like a mountain to climb. When in Darkness, we experience a lot of emotional suffering and the future seems bleak. We feel vulnerable and disconnected from any positive influence or potential. We may even tell ourselves we are a lost cause. 'What's the point?'

Thoughts: 'I can't handle this. It's too much. I'm useless.'

Emotions: despair, apathy, hopelessness.

Body sensations: heavy chest, dull stomach ache, overall numbness.

Parent behavioural patterns: You are likely to withdraw, disconnect, feel overwhelmed and unable to provide support to your family as you struggle to motivate yourself, let alone anyone else. You will probably have a real sense of feeling depleted and running on empty.

Child behavioural patterns: Your child may completely withdraw any interest in their education and may even refuse to go to school, or not engage with your home education. They will likely be apathetic, showing signs of distress and shutting down emotionally.

In Darkness, your judgement is often focused on shrouding yourself in shame, guilt and regret.

2. Dimness: Unstable energy – drained

In the Dimness state, you have a sense of being stuck in Groundhog Day. Unable to move forward or always finding yourself back at square one. Frustration and resignation kick in; this is how life is for you. Your energy levels are low and you engage half-heartedly, often setting yourself up to fail in unconscious ways. You might go through the motions without a real commitment to the outcome because you don't believe you can win or have success. It's hard to be enthusiastic when it feels as though you are forcing things, putting on a brave face but ultimately being ineffective.

Thoughts: 'I don't know if I can do this. It's too hard. I'll do it tomorrow.'

Emotions: pessimism, frustration, resignation.

Body sensations: tension in shoulders and neck, furrowed brow, mild chest pressure.

Parent behavioural patterns: You may start to micromanage and hover over your child with frustration, impatience and judgement. You may criticise or show a lack of confidence in them, which reflects your own doubts about yourself.

Child behavioural patterns: They are reluctant to put in any effort if they can't see the point and they get annoyed easily, giving up at the slightest hurdle. They push back at your attempts to encourage them to be more positive and shut down any offer of support.

In Dimness, your judgement might be focused on others and external circumstances. You are where you are because of everyone else, and the broken system. This is outside-in thinking, and it traps you as a victim, leaving you powerless to do anything about your situation.

3. Glimmer: Flickering energy – neutral

Being in the more neutral energy of Glimmer is like standing at a crossroads. You have a choice to make, but any moments of clarity and optimism are quickly met with doubt and hesitation. You don't trust yourself to make the right choice. 'What if I get it wrong?' So you become indecisive and stay stuck, telling yourself you'll do it tomorrow, that you need more information, or wish someone else would decide for you. In this signature, you are probably the most motivated to do something about your child's disengagement as you'll have a tinge of curiosity – 'Maybe I could do a better job' – which gets you looking for solutions. This is a crucial Lights Off signature to harness for growth because if you can shift your energy into its Lights On counterpart, Glow, you'll have success.

Thoughts: 'Maybe I can do something about this, but what if I fail?'

Emotions: uncertainty, doubt, curiosity (curiosity is the gateway to the Lights On signatures).

Body sensations: fluttering in the stomach, dullness in the chest, occasional warmth in the heart when curiosity and hope kick in, light-headedness.

Parent behavioural patterns: The pull of curiosity in this signature is enough to get you excited to explore new strategies or approaches, so you initiate some action. As you hit resistance, you tell yourself it hasn't worked, again, and you withdraw completely. Your inconsistency is frustrating to you and your child and gives mixed messages to everyone in your family.

Child behavioural patterns: Your child's engagement is inconsistent, which is frustrating. You can see their wasted potential just below the surface. If only they could focus and find the motivation to keep going. Like you, in this signature, they are not confident they can achieve or succeed, and they seek a lot of validation, encouragement and reassurance from others.

Being in Glimmer signifies massive potential for growth and stability if you engage the power of choice. Fear of failure is a defining characteristic which leads to a nervousness to try, and second-guessing what you 'should' be doing. When used intentionally for recovery and growth, it is a powerful Lights Off signature for learning. You can still think clearly, respond to stress adaptively and enjoy life's experiences with a renewed perspective. The shift into Glow is a thought away, once you are ready.

4. Glow: Steady energy – invigorated

The Glow state marks the entry into the Lights On signatures, where you have a more consistent sense of optimism and contentment. Your energy is steady and you have a warm, invigorating feeling that motivates you to keep putting in the effort and engaging in learning and life. You have a balanced outlook and can meet bite-size challenges with a hopeful, positive and proactive attitude. You have clarity on the way forward (you know which fork in the road to take) and you genuinely feel motivated, interested and enthusiastic to take action. You definitely can move the needle forward in this signature, but as it is a lovely place to be, it can quickly become your comfort zone, along with Glimmer.

Thoughts: 'I can see how I can do this.'

Emotions: optimism, passion, contentment.

Body sensations: Warm, expanding sensation in the chest, steady warmth in the heart.

Parent behavioural patterns: You have a positive and supportive attitude towards your family, and encourage them to explore and learn through their passions. You can see what lights them up and give them time and space to be Lights On. You offer constructive feedback (critique not criticism) and enjoy celebrating your micro-wins together. You make sure your child feels confident and motivated to learn, and you support them beyond their comfort zone because you are comfortable stepping beyond yours.

Child behavioural patterns: Your child engages with learning and life more consistently, and responds positively to your support and encouragement.

They are willing to try new things and, overall, they approach learning with an optimistic outlook. They are Lights On!

There are subtle differences between Glow and Glimmer because your head and heart are expressing themselves at the same time. Which one you listen to will determine whether you are in Lights Off (Glimmer), or Lights On (Glow). Ultimately, if your heart desires more and you are hungry for the thrill and impact that comes with growth, then you can choose to ascend upwards. Why would you not?! Many parents feel that, if they settle in the comfort of Glow, they will lose their motivation to achieve more in their lives. Getting real clarity on your vision, which we will do in Chapter 8, will build in more motivation unless you intentionally choose comfort over growth.

5. Brilliance: Vibrant and energised

In the signature of Brilliance, you feel a vibrant energy buzzing through your body. Your passion and enthusiasm drive your actions and you feel a strong internal power that pulls you forward to achieve your goals. Your creativity feels unlimited and you begin to truly flourish. You feel lively, inspired, motivated and fulfilled. Your confidence is high and you readily commit to autographing your work with excellence. This is a signature where you can get stuff done with ease and flow. As you tune into Brilliance, you hone your creativity and nurture your growing intuition to harness your passion and purpose in sustainable ways. Your energy to take continual action is fuelled by your curiosity, passion and purpose, rather than a fleeting desire or a momentary feeling of invincibility, as in Glow. This is a sustainable drive which turns your dreams into reality as you embrace challenges and take intentional and inspired action to step fully into your life's quest. Obstacles become adventures to navigate in creative ways, and failures provide healthy learning curves.

Thoughts: 'I have what it takes to make this work. It's hard, but I'm going for it.'

Emotions: passion, enthusiasm, gratitude, inspiration.

Body sensations: strong, consistent warmth in the heart, persistent smile or glow, sense of empowerment in the solar plexus.

Parent behavioural patterns: You are an inspiring role model for your family, friends and work colleagues. You have a great enthusiasm and passion for learning and you share the sense that 'anything is possible' with those around you. You can create engaging and dynamic learning experiences for your family and you nurture curiosity, courage and creativity, which makes learning a joyful and exciting process for everyone.

Child behavioural patterns: Your child demonstrates high levels of engagement, enthusiasm and a strong desire to learn and succeed. They use their initiative, explore their creativity and are open to taking risks, autographing their work with excellence and have a commitment to their own vision. They continually seek to broaden their knowledge and gain additional insights related to their interests. Their passion for learning is evident. They are proactive and excited to learn. They are sparky, independent, happy, courageous, resilient and bold.

Brilliance marks the entrance to your truest human potential and opens the door to Radiance.

6. Radiance: Unified energy – harmonised

The essence of Radiance is a profound sense of peace, joy, love, gratitude and freedom. Energy flows effortlessly and harmoniously, and you feel serene and balanced. You feel abundant, free from the constraints of your mental, emotional and physical boundaries. This is where you feel limitless and have a deep appreciation for life, as well as a feeling of being connected to something bigger than yourself. It's the entry point to spiritual growth, where actions are guided by love and clarity, and you have an enduring sense of being fulfilled. This is the signature where you truly believe 'all is well' and that you are 'exactly where you are meant to be'. It is also when you have a deep inner trust that you are living the life you were born to live.

Thoughts: 'I am amazing. I love being me. I can do anything.'

Emotions: joy, love, gratitude, freedom.

Body sensations: light, buoyant feeling throughout the body, deep, sustained warmth in the heart, sense of clarity and tranquillity in the mind.

Parent behavioural patterns: You bring a serene and balanced approach to leading your family. You create a nurturing and harmonious culture within your home, and you inspire your child and everyone around you. You are calm and confident and believe in yourself and them. You are consistent and peaceful, and you encourage a love for learning with ease. You radiate a magnetic energy which attracts people to you, and you have plenty of evidence that what you want in life is coming your way. In fact, you have all you need; right here, right now, all is well.

Child behavioural patterns: Your child has a deep love for learning and engages fully in the process. They often go above and beyond what is required of them, diving deep into the vast field of potentiality available to them. They see opportunity and they take it, knowing they will fail forward repeatedly on the path to success. They have a balanced, joyful attitude towards learning and life. It is beautiful to watch them take full ownership of who they were born to be and to see them love who they are.

This signature has proved to be the most difficult for parents to connect with at first. If this one feels elusive, it simply highlights an area for growth, which means you have something magical waiting for you!

Your unique signatures are key to your child's love of learning

I appreciate this is a lot to take in. You might even feel a bit Lights Off that my approach to re-engaging your child and leading them to love learning really does start with you. You no doubt already feel responsible for their happiness, and feel guilty you are not doing 'enough'. To let go of the old-school paradigm can feel daunting. While many parents love the sound of my passion-led learning approach, not everyone is ready for the internal transformation that comes with it. Only you can decide if the time is right for you to use your child's disengagement for your own personal and professional development, too. I invite you to see this as a great opportunity to rediscover the passions and purpose that you might have lost touch with since becoming a parent.

Take Chris, for example. After our first call, he realised his dream and passion for creating music were packed away in cardboard boxes. The fact that his music studio wasn't set up, yet, had become a convenient excuse to not make music. As a dad and business owner, he was telling himself it wasn't a priority. He didn't have time. When he understood that, if he wanted to see his son and two daughters feel the joy that comes with heart-led learning, then he and his wife needed to role model what that looked like. He took immediate action, unpacked the boxes, set up his music studio and began creating again after two years of procrastinating. Turns out his eleven-year-old son also loves making music and began composing original songs, which felt so much better than playing video games all the time.

Using the Lights On spectrum to shine a spotlight on your own readiness and willingness to learn is a complete game changer for your family. It is a beautiful and harmonious way to learn and lead your lives, and it results in a lot more connection within your family, too.

Unpacking the cultural DNA of education

If you consider yourself an innovative and progressive thinker, and you've been doing personal development for years, this will all feel familiar inner work. However, you might still have some old-school thinking hardwired about what education 'should' be like. As Ivana, who was amazed by how much old-school thinking made an appearance at the start of her family's Lights On Learning adventure:

'It has been a big week for us! My old self would have so easily brushed it away as a little one!

'Andrew and I have been navigating through the Lights On portal. We had a sense we were embarking on a massive shift by deregistering our nine-year-old twin sons from the school system to follow the Lights On Learning approach.

'Every step we took forward, we were faced with old-school thinking. It was incredible to observe this… like sparks going off. Whenever we were opening our mouths what came out was so obviously old-school and not even something we've consciously thought to be true. It became obvious how quickly we were shutting down the grand ideas our children had.

'So we decided to take the focus away from our children and allow us space and time for our mindset to shift. This of course brought more "gifts" to see some more old thinking and insecurities as we realised we are going to fully need to embrace inside-out learning ourselves, too, to create such a different culture in our home.

'There is no hiding anymore. This feels so fundamentally different from old-school thinking we've had.'

I love Ivana's willingness to see where her growth lies and to grab the opportunity to learn and grow exponentially so her family could too. This is the offer Lights On Learning presents. It is an exciting path of personal growth and development for you, too. Your child's disengagement is your biggest reason to reconnect with who you were born to be and to realise that what you think, feel and do affects your experience of life on a profound level.

As you get clarity within your personal Lights On spectrum, you will shine the spotlight on so many growth opportunities. You will likely ask yourself, 'Why didn't I know this sooner?' Like I did and like every parent I've worked with who has become ready to ceremoniously burn, shred or rip up their old-school rules and cast a new vision for their family's educational adventure.

As Rachel shared,

> 'I am very excited about the in-depth descriptions. They have changed the way I view my own Lights On practice. Powerful! We, the leaders of our families, are learning to navigate up and down the spectrum, rather than aiming for a destination. It has made it so clear which signature I am in, where I want to be and what's limiting me.'

For Ruth's family, having an increased awareness of the Lights On spectrum also made an immediate impact: 'It's opening up conversation and giving us a common language. We're using it as a connection tool. We sit together and have a chat about the last twenty-four hours, which has made getting ready for school noticeably easier.'

Felicity also gained so much insight in the first two weeks of joining our community:

> 'These last two weeks of tracking have been really helpful. Gosh, I have a lot of unhelpful thoughts! I'm really noticing when I start to feel an increase in pressure in my head or chest, I can stop and see which thought has come in, that's stopping me from being me.'

Over the next two chapters, we're going to use your child's disengagement and your vision for them to explore your habits of thoughts, emotions and feelings so you can get the first draft of your personal Lights On spectrum. Are you ready to become a sparky and dive into your neurocircuitry? Let's begin with your Lights Off signatures. What are you making your child's disengagement mean – about them, and you?

6
Your Lights Off Cascade

The first time I remember thinking, 'I can't do this, it's too hard,' I was seven years old, standing on a wooden pole three metres up a 500-year-old yew tree. I was with my father, who was persuading me to jump onto a swing that went across a pond. The swing seat didn't reach the tree fully, so I had to balance, lean out, hold the rope, jump and land on the thin stick seat. If I was successful, I would swing down across the pond and soar high up into the sky. If I missed, I would crash onto the ground and be dragged down the steep bank into the water.

I just couldn't do it. I was too scared. I kept thinking that I would miss the seat. Despite my dad's patience and reassurance that it was safe to jump, I kept saying, 'I can't do this.'

'Yes, you can,' he replied.

'I can't.'

After what seemed like forever, my dad helped me down from the tree. I hadn't been brave enough to swing.

I felt sad that I hadn't done it. The fear at the time was too much. My legs were too wobbly. I felt sick with nerves. I was scared.

I so wanted to do it, like my older sister Jane could. Later that day, I asked my dad to sit me on the seat and throw me off the edge. I knew that if I could experience what it felt like to soar across the pond, I would be able to do it on my own.

So that's what we did. It was exhilarating! I loved the feeling in my stomach as I swung up high and, for a micro-moment, felt like I was suspended in mid-air before I swung back across the pond again.

I climbed straight back up and jumped on again, on my own. My father gave me the leap of faith to believe that I could do it, as he would on many occasions throughout my life. I went on to spend the rest of my childhood learning the art of rope swing tricks, moving from 'I can't' to 'I can'. From Lights Off to Lights On.

This neural network – 'I can't do it, it's too hard' – was the first big Lights Off belief that I rewired forty-two years later. It was powerful to realise that it had been playing on a loop in my subconscious mind. In a powerful, deep-healing meditation, I had a vision of my seven-year-old self standing up in that yew tree at that exact moment. Instead of my dad next to me, I, as an adult, was there. 'You can do this. In fact, you *do* do it. You go on to do so many hard things in your life that you could not even imagine. Jump. You can do this. You're going to love it.' As I began to emerge from the meditation, all I could hear, on a loop, was the thought, 'I can do this. I can do this. I can do this.' Whatever it is you set your heart, mind and skills to, you can do, too.

I share my story about the rope swing to highlight that, when it comes to rewiring your Lights Off circuitry, you don't have to look for traumatic events or cast any blame, shame or guilt in any direction. When you come across a Lights Off neural circuit, simply acknowledge that you have this thought and write it down. Ask if it still serves you, and then choose to keep this circuitry in place or rewire it. As you witness, process and rewire your Lights Off circuits, you shift out of judgement and lead yourself and others from a more compassionate place. This inbuilt healing element enables you to change the legacy for your child, their children and generations to come.

Lights Off thoughts are normal

It is always a huge relief for every parent I work with to know that negative thought patterns are normal and we all have them. To help you gain insight into what they might look like, in relation to being a parent, I've composed some examples based on patterns that emerge from my work as a neurocoach. As you read them, make a note if any resonate with you. Notice if any trigger an emotional charge in your body. The same cautionary note in the previous chapter applies. If you start feeling too agitated, take a breath, get up and move, and tune into a thought that always makes you smile.

- 'I feel I have let my family down. I make promises and then don't follow through.'

- 'I am scared. I don't know who I am. I don't have anything I enjoy doing. I feel I have to make everyone else happy. What about me?'

- 'I feel resentful. My dream has been snatched away from me and I'll never get there. What's wrong with me? I've failed to make it work – as a mum and in my career.'

- 'I feel frustrated. I am such a go-getter but my child isn't interested in anything. They have no ambition or belief in themselves. I feel disappointed that I haven't done enough. I've failed him and I feel shame around that.'

- 'My family brings out the worst in me. I always feel like I'm not important. I'm not heard and not listened to.'

- 'I feel like no one understands. I feel helpless. That I can't change anything.'

- 'I feel scared, alone and overwhelmed. This is too big. I've failed because I can't hack it. I am not who I thought I was.'

- 'I had this vision of being a hands-on, stay-at-home mum, but everything feels dull. I've lost myself along the way. I feel sad that I'm expected to be more than what I am and I'm not good enough.'

- 'I might not be able to do it all, so I lower my expectations. I feel ashamed of who I am. I want to walk away as I'm not sure I can do this.'

These are powerful Lights Off thought patterns, which I am sure you can see would make anyone feel disheartened or disempowered about leading their children to love learning. With these thoughts in play, it will feel too big a mountain to climb and you won't believe you can do it. Even as I wrote them, they made me feel sad that so many parents have this negative self-talk but are not aware of it.

Thinking and believing 'I am not good enough' does not mean it is true. It does, however, cause you to feel and act as though it were true, and it becomes a self-fulfilling prophecy as we've seen with Ollie, Oscar, Ruby, James and Max. What they, and we, believe about ourselves determines our self-perception, identity and the results we get in life. Change our thinking and we change the outcomes that become available to us. Importantly, we change how we feel. From Lights Off to Lights On. When we do that, we transform what is possible for us and the people around us.

Lights Off is a reactionary state and until you uncover your Lights Off signatures, you won't know why you feel the way you do. The more self-aware of your Lights Off signatures you and your family become, the quicker you will be able to rewire and upgrade your learning circuitry and access Brilliance and Radiance on demand, as you'll learn in Part Three.

Getting up close and personal with your Lights Off circuits

Through my work, as a neurocoach, I have seen how many of us find ourselves in the dark, lonely and scary place as we cascade into Darkness. Some of us land there momentarily, and some of us for prolonged periods, lost and disconnected from who we were born to be. Therefore, when our children become Lights Off, triggered by their own disconnection with learning, it is like a mirror reflecting our truth. We look into their eyes, full of boredom, resignation, apathy and self-loathing, and we see the sadness, fear and unfulfilled, wasted potential we feel within ourselves. 'What if we can't fix this? What if we don't have what it takes to lead our family to be happy and fulfilled? What if we are, in fact, a bad parent?' It feels real and deeply triggering because we can't bear our children to feel like this too, living a disconnected, unfulfilled life in the shadows.

So, let's just accept it is hugely triggering when our children disengage from learning or lose their spark. It is a normal, healthy reaction to feel as though we are failing when they are not happy. We want to protect them, make life better for them, and fix their problems as fast as we can. It can feel great to rage against the education system, but I don't recommend it. I hit my head against the brick wall of the school many times before I realised it was a futile, unrewarding and counterproductive strategy. When you accept responsibility that you are the best person to change your child's attitude to learning, you can respond to their disengagement in a new way. Because, let's be honest, how successful do you think you'll be trying to solve your child's disengagement with Lights Off signatures running all the time?

We're going to use your child's disengagement as the situational trigger to flush out your thoughts, feelings and emotions within your three Lights Off signatures (Darkness, Dimness and Glimmer). I suggest you get yourself a dedicated Lights Off journal to write down your thoughts on paper. If, like many parents, you feel uncomfortable committing your thoughts to paper, write them down to stop the self-rumination in your head and then shred, burn or compost the pages.

Decide in advance what to do if you start to feel unsettled, or even scared by the thoughts you uncover. I recommend you immediately ask yourself, 'What am I thinking?' and write it down to get it out of your head. Then take some deep breaths, play music that lights you up, or go for a walk outside to help you shift intentionally into Glow, the Lights On comfort zone.

Use the template and question prompts below to capture your thoughts, feelings and emotions around your child's disengagement. Start filling in the template at Darkness and work your way up to Glimmer to embed the habit of energetically shifting from Lights Off to Lights On.

Your emotions are what you experience within your body, such as anger or fear. Your feelings are the mental interpretation of that energy in motion, such as feeling angry or scared. For example, the emotion might be fear, the feeling is being scared and the thought might be 'I'm not safe.' As you begin to explore your Lights Off signatures, you will get a clear indication of how your thoughts, feelings and emotions are limiting you in every aspect of your life.

- What are your thoughts about your child's current attitude to learning? What do you feel when you think these thoughts?

- What are the emotions you experience when you think about their current/potential attitude to learning?

- Where do you feel these emotions in your body?

My unique Lights Off signatures			
Lights Off signatures	Thoughts and feelings	Emotions	Where I feel it in my body
Glimmer			
Dimness			
Darkness			

↑
Start here!

A few layers deeper

Your Lights Off signatures will ensure you see everything that is 'not enough' with yourself or your child.

It becomes all about what you, or they, can't do or are not doing. You are possibly creating a Lights Off version of them in your mind that doesn't even exist, and future casting their downfall. This puts incredible pressure and energy of urgency on you both to 'do better', to 'be different', to 'be happy'.

'What if I can't "fix" it? What will that mean for their education, for their future, for their life? What will it say about me?' Only you get to decide what it means about you, so let's find out.

Use the following sentence starter to explore your worst-case scenario: 'When I think about my child being disengaged and not caring about their education, I worry that…'

When you get your initial answer, ask yourself, 'If that were to happen, what am I making this mean about them and me?' Keep going until you feel like you have uncovered the real fear. Here are some honest Lights Off cascades from parents inside my community:

> 'When I think about my child being disengaged and not caring about their education, I worry they will live unfulfilled lives and not be happy. There is also a grumbling sense this might reflect on me… that how they are in their adult life will be an indicator of how I parented them. I feel a sense of grief and regret if this were to be the

case. That I didn't do enough. It's a heart cry of "I tried my hardest. I did my best! Please understand me and see that I'm not a bad person."'

'When I think about my daughter being disengaged and not caring about her education, I worry she will end up making some incredibly poor choices. That she will become pregnant at the age of nineteen with someone who isn't compatible or has little ability to love her. She will live a life of missed opportunity because she couldn't see the point in trying and has ruined her life! If I am honest, that means we have failed as parents.'

'When I think about my child being disengaged and not caring about their education, I worry that I have failed them. That I am a failure. That they will fail in life. That we're not good enough, not significant, not worthy of love, belonging or life.'

Time and time again, when a parent follows the trail of their Lights Off circuitry, it leads to a deep fear of failure and letting their child down. When they acknowledge this fear, they can lead from a more self-aware, empowered place. When they don't know it is there, they are stuck in reactive mode being triggered over and over again, trying every solution under the sun, with nothing changing. Lights Off!

Our Lights Off signatures are sneaky, but when you uncover them, they are your direct signal to what needs rewiring. While you will no doubt begin to discover many Lights Off circuits from this point forward, you will also learn the tools to create that 3:1 positivity ratio that Barbara Fredrickson gifted us. To become Lights On more of the time, you have to be more intentional about activating your Lights On signatures. In the next chapter, we'll develop a clear vision for your new passion-led educational strategy and use this to prime in your Lights On circuits.

7
Casting Your Lights On Vision

My daughter chose to go back to school at age eleven. A couple of years later, aged thirteen, she began requesting more days at home. When I received a letter about her attendance, I thought: 'Bring it on!' If I was accountable for her physically being in school, then they were accountable for her mental wellbeing while she was there. I organised a meeting with her head of year. Esme shared openly how she felt the culture within the school wasn't conducive to her mental health. When asked what she needed to come into school and feel good, Esme began her negotiation!

She wanted time to explore her passion – writing. She walked out of that meeting having completely flexed the system, dropping five subjects and gaining ten hours of freedom over the two-week timetable. Over the next two years of secondary school, she dived deep into her Heartset, Mindset and Skillset, and independently studied for a psychology GCSE and an Extended Project Qualification (EPQ). She also ran a primary research project about the importance of student autonomy in note-taking, which influenced decisions at a senior leadership level. At the leavers' assembly, the principal gave her the graduate award, commending her as a changemaker who does the right thing when no one is looking.

Esme's EPQ explored the question: does engaging in a passion impact mental wellbeing? She explored how passion gives us meaning and purpose and, as it comes from within, is accessible to all. She researched Geelong Grammar School and their Positive Education model developed with Martin Seligman, known as the father of the positive psychology discipline.[31] My neurodiverse Australian nephew, Finn, spent a year at Geelong in their Timbertop programme, so I witnessed the power of their approach up close. It was a tough growth year for him, but he absolutely shone in a way that was authentic for him. When his mum asked him what he felt he had achieved he replied, 'I know who I am now.'

---

31 Geelong Grammar School, 'What is Positive Education?' (no date), www.ggs.vic.edu.au/learning/wellbeing/what-is-positive-education, accessed 25 August 2024

Seligman's research highlights how wellbeing and learning are interconnected. We simply can't separate the two, and why would we? Here's an extract from Esme's EPQ about what happens when we disconnect our Heartset and take away the thing that lights us up:

> 'If engaging in a passion brings positive effects, are there negative effects of not engaging in a passion? A study by Csikszentmihalyi (cited in Pink, 2011 p129) found that when participants were instructed to remove all sources of flow from their lives for the duration of the study, there were significant impacts on their ability to function mentally. By the end of the first day, participants reported feeling sluggish about their behaviour. They began to experience headaches, had difficulty concentrating and felt either sleepy or too agitated to sleep. After only forty-eight hours, Csikszentmihalyi wrote that: "The general deterioration in mood was so advanced that prolonging the experiment would have been inadvisable." The results of this study suggest that passion has a much higher importance than just being an easy way to increase mental wellbeing. It seems it is actually imperative to prevent mental deterioration.'[32]

---

32 D Pink, *Drive: The surprising truth about what motivates us* (Riverhead Books, 2009)

Wow! Remove flow from our lives and our mental health declines rapidly. Csikszentmihalyi's work on happiness, as an internal state to cultivate, is instrumental to my thinking behind Lights On Learning. He defines flow as 'A state in which people are so involved in an activity that nothing else seems to matter.'[33] That thing you love to do, that you want to wake up every morning to explore, that fast tracks you into the 'zone'? Well, that counts. In my words, our passion lights us up, sparks our learning circuitry and provides us with an unwavering mental, emotional and physical connection to learning. It gives us purpose, meaning and intrinsic motivation, and fast-tracks us into Brilliance and Radiance.

Passion-led learning changes the game

Even just a couple of hours a week of engaging in self-led passion projects can give us a sense of personal power, freedom and autonomy, as it did for my daughter. When our children activate their Lights On signatures, they show up differently. A great example of this is how some parents would struggle to get their children up and out the door for school, except on Thursdays. This was the day their children came to our Digital Lounge after-school sessions. On these mornings, their children were up and ready, no doubt

---

33 M Csikszentmihalyi, *Flow: The psychology of happiness* (Rider, 2002)

anticipating the reward of having time later that day to explore, experiment and create through their passion for technology and digital wizardry.

Here's what Shonogh Pilgrim, CEO of Whole Education, shared about seeing her students learn in this way when we worked together in 2017:

> 'Seeing the students tapping into the core of who they are, being permitted to believe in themselves has been amazing. Every single one of them is desperate to be freed to push themselves further than people around them have ever imagined. Not just in the narrow realms judged acceptable by a traditional academic-is-everything-obsessed society. They know they need their English and maths. They want that to be the foundation, not the limit. I am confident that when you give people control, they don't settle for mediocrity unless you do your best to convince them that is their limit!'

Absolutely. When your child feels passion and enthusiasm for learning, they will become driven, motivated, energised and inspired. They will also feel the educational and health benefits that come with the power of having a deep love for learning.

Love in the Lights On spectrum

Barbara Fredrickson refers to love as our supreme emotion that affects our physical health, vitality and wellbeing. It is an energising life force that influences us at a cellular level, changes our mind and broadens our perception.[34] I've discovered that, when it comes to learning, love changes everything. It opens us up to emotional and spiritual growth and brings in the joy of creating with ease and flow. As a community, exploring our Lights On signatures in-depth, we have discovered that love is a harmonising force. It gifts us a sense of wholeness, fulfilment and inner peace. Here are some insights about how parents experience the nuances of love within their Lights On spectrum:

> 'I think love is in both Brilliance and Radiance in different ways. The love in Brilliance is sparked by excitement – because for me, Brilliance is when I'm feeling motivated and inspired. It's a generous sort of love, if that makes sense. I'm feeling excited about things and as a consequence, I pour love outwards onto other people in my life. Love in Radiance is a contented, peaceful, yet still joyful sort of love.' (Charlotte)

> 'Brilliance brings gratitude and love in an excited and bubbly way, like a child in flow

---

[34] B Fredrickson, *Love 2.0: Creating happiness and health in moments of connection* (Plume, 2014)

with their passion. An earthly and bodily love. Radiance brings a type of love which encompasses gratitude, it's infinite and feels like peace and stillness. It goes beyond the mind and thought. It's a more spiritual love.' (Sarah)

'The love in Brilliance is like new love, infatuation love. So much energy and excitement, bubbling over with love. The love in Radiance is peaceful, secure, deep, long-lasting love.' (Felicity)

'To me, the feeling of love for others is in Brilliance but the love for myself is more aligned with Radiance.' (Claire)

Even without Fredrickson's scientific deep-dive into the power of love, it's common-sense, for most of us, to want our children to love learning. When they do, and they become Lights On more often, we can see it is healthier for them. Mentally, emotionally, physically and spiritually, they benefit. Having the power of love explored and expressed within your family immediately changes what is possible for you all. When you know how to calibrate to love and infuse it throughout your Lights On spectrum, you discover inner peace, calm and a sense of fulfilment as you enter an expanded state of awareness. Even when you become Lights Off, you can experience it through an attunement of love, because your ability to regulate your emotional state, through increased resilience, allows you to feel all the emotions available.

Having a real love of learning

Even introducing the word 'love' in connection to learning can create an energetic shift, as Jo discovered:

> 'I have been reflecting on the word learning. When I talk about the love of learning, my heart sings. It is the one thing I have not swayed from since having my children. I want them to be lifelong learners, who love learning. It feels light, natural, playful and a place where Radiance can flourish. When I take out the word love and just have the word learning, I have a different feeling. A pull towards old-school thinking. My lights dim. It feels heavy, imposed and a necessity.'

Let's take advantage of the L-word to spark a conversation with your family. Here are some questions to explore together to see if it shifts them to reimagine how learning can be for them:

- What does learning mean to us as a family?
- What would have to change for us to love learning?

- What would we be exploring, discovering and doing?
- How would we feel?
- What would be possible if we truly loved learning, even when faced with a challenge?

'To love learning – it would feel there was no right or wrong way to do it, that it is expansive and multisensory. It can be done in any way and there would be curiosity. Failure wouldn't matter as there would be no judgement.
It would come from a curiosity to deepen knowing or a desire to serve rather than just a need for knowledge.' (Nicole)

'Now I've found what I'm passionate about, I love learning. I feel like a sponge soaking everything in and growing with every new bit of information. I love it when information from different sources connects or changes my perspective slightly.' (Claire)

Coding a vision blueprint for your family

I hope this little exploration into the power of love excites you to bring Lights On Learning into your home. You can start simply by doing more of what lights you all up, exploring your switches and using tools like the learning carousel and draft critique to create a Lights On feedback loop.

When you are ready, you can be intentional and strategic about encoding love into your Lights On signatures to lead by example and create a positivity resonance that ripples through your family.[35] We've seen how quickly a family transforms when a parent takes the lead to become Lights On first, and Nadia, a mother in my community, named this the 'Lights On effect'.

Time to attune your vision blueprint to what your heart desires for your family.

Step one: Create your big dream

Read the following question out loud: 'If I could wave a magic wand, what would I wish for myself and my family and the world around me?'

Then close your eyes, quieten your mind and listen to your heart.

- What is it you see/sense/imagine?
- What do you feel when you tune into that reality?

---

35 B Fredrickson, *Positivity* (Harmony Books, 2009)

CASTING YOUR LIGHTS ON VISION

- What thoughts would help you feel that, in this present moment?
- Who are you being as you lead your family to that place?
- What are you doing, day-to-day, to make this dream come true?

You want your vision statement to be simple enough to declare first thing in the morning when you wake up. It needs to be short, punchy and memorable. Most importantly, it needs to light you up. Take your answers and try to simplify them down to one powerful sentence that excites you, using the following sentence starter:

'I see a world where my family _____.'

Here are some of the powerful vision statements from my community:

'My vision is for my family to be connected, happy and fulfilled, able to play fully in the world.' (Jo)

'We are a family who use our interests and talents to live a purposeful and meaningful life.' (Nicole)

'My family have the courage to follow their dreams with joy.' (Charlotte)

LIGHTS ON LEARNING

Step two: Supercharge your vision with love

Next, you want to infuse your vision statement with love.

Take a moment to imagine your child doing something that lights them up. Close your eyes and picture them highly engaged, exploring beyond their comfort zone, overcoming obstacles. Imagine them tuning into their passions, purpose and potential every day, just like when they were toddlers learning to walk, talk, dance and sing.

Sparky. Energised. Radiant.

Resilient. Courageous. Bold.

Feels great to imagine them like this, doesn't it?

Now tune into a memory where you saw their Brilliance shine through. You could see it in their eyes, their lights were on. See, sense or feel yourself looking at them, and allow an incredible inner warmth to glow within your heart like you could almost cry, it feels so good. Use a slow, deep breath to anchor in what it feels like to see them in their element, being their authentic self. As you feel the power of your Lights On emotions – love, gratitude, joy – smile on the inside and cast your vision into the world by declaring it loud and proud.

If you haven't quite reached your vision statement yet, feel the Lights On emotions and read mine: 'I see a world where all children love learning.'

Does that feel good to imagine that reality? It does for me and focuses my attention because the truth is, your child, and every child, was born to flourish, and we're here to make sure that can happen by choice, not circumstance.

Step three: Code your Lights On signatures

Now you have the beginnings of your vision blueprint, you want to code your Lights On signatures to align with it, so you can step into your vision today. I like to do visioning as though I'm in that reality, rather than holding it at arm's length as something to arrive at. For example, for my children to love learning today, what needs to happen? They need to know what lights them up, have plenty of evidence of what they can achieve using their switch, and have support to continually build their resilience to face the challenges life will bring them. I do not want to wait for that to be our reality. Can you see how simple we can make this?

Use the questions and template below to get your first draft of thoughts, feelings and emotions you experience in Glow, Brilliance and Radiance. Remember to

LIGHTS ON LEARNING

start at Glow to continue to build the habit of energetically ascending to Radiance.

- What do you feel when you think of your vision for your family to love learning?
- What thoughts do you have when you imagine this as your reality?
- What emotions are you tuning into?
- Where do you feel it in your body?

My Lights On signatures

Lights On signatures	Thoughts and feelings	Emotions	Where I feel it in my body
Radiance			
Brilliance			
Glow			

↑
Start here!

As with any Lights On Learning the key to success is taking action and getting your first draft. Your vision doesn't need to be perfect, as it will evolve, as Katrin shares:

> 'My vision for home educating has grown bigger through Lights On Learning. We have moved from more structured learning to passion-led learning. My vision is to move to a space where everyone in my family is learning with their lights fully switched on and to their fullest potential.'

She is walking in her vision daily. It has been incredible to see Katrin's family grow as learners under her Lights On leadership. Her three children know their switches, they learn through them every day, and they have incredible portfolios that showcase what they are achieving with their Heartset, Mindset and Skillset fully connected. Her most recent vision is simple, concise and impactful: 'We are a family of changemakers impacting the world for good.' They certainly are, and to support their changemaker quest to make a difference, here's a mini-project Katrin designed for her family to create a discussion about how their heart-brain connection affects their outcomes.

A LIGHTS ON LEARNING PROJECT
Brought to you by Katrin and her family

Introducing the Lights On concept to your family can feel like a daunting task at first and you might find yourself thinking...

- Will my children engage?
- Will they 'get it'?
- What if they're not interested?

I've been there, too, which is why I wanted to share a fun and engaging way I've used to introduce and explore what Lights On means to us. I hope it will inspire you to find creative ways with your family.

The tool we used arrived one day quite unexpectedly by post in the form of a trial STEM box – a spin art machine!

My son, who has a maker/artist/engineer switch, loved putting it together and immediately started experimenting with it. The resulting spin art was fascinating as well as beautiful. I suddenly saw the potential for explaining Lights On and Off with this STEM project. As a family, we've found when our heart is connected with our brain there is a direct link to our creative output.

The spinning machine was perfect to illustrate this. You could adjust the connection between the motor and the battery pack to change the speed of the turning table. A direct connection resulted in the spinning table turning at high speed, and a connection with resistors slowed the spinning table down.

We got curious – what if the battery pack would represent the heart and the motor of the spinning table the brain?

How would the way these two are connected affect the outcome of the artwork?

We started with a direct connection, then we added more and more resistors and watched how this impacted the spin art:

Lights On *Lights Off*

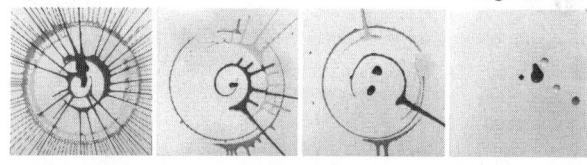

The four different outcomes still hang on our wall in the dining room and remind us daily to switch our lights on to impact the world through a fully aligned heart and mindset.

In the second step, we explored some thoughts and feelings to dive deeper into our understanding of each of the different stages and created a poster.

I would like to invite you to experiment with this yourself. If you don't have access to a spin art machine, how could you use your creative switches to explain and explore what Lights On and Off mean to your family?

Trust your intuition and remember, with Lights On Learning, there is no right or wrong way!

Amazing! Katrin's family took it one step further and also made a short film. This is Lights On Learning at its best. The simple roadmap? Take something you are curious to learn about. Use your family's switches to explore and experiment. Present your discoveries in a unique, creative, tangible expression. Get excited about where this will lead you to learn and grow in extraordinary ways.

When you take up adventures using this Lights On Learning roadmap, you will encounter challenges along the way that lead to growth. This is where your Lights On spectrum comes in as a compass and a calibration tool, to keep you focused, on track and moving forward.

Recognising the important role that being Lights Off plays in the pursuit of being Lights On is a game changer. Instead of this thought pattern – 'Why are we doing this? What is the point? It doesn't feel good' – we can shift to 'This doesn't feel good, but if I can figure it out, then it's going to feel great.' A moment of emotional discomfort creates a big payoff, as a conversation I had with one extremely high-achieving thirteen-year-old highlights. He was struggling to do Oscar's Impossible Triangle activity but wouldn't give up. I said to him, 'How does it feel to be inspired by a six-year-old's capabilities?' He replied, without looking up, 'I'm not inspired, I'm annoyed by him!' and kept going to get a final draft he was satisfied with.

In Part Three, we're going to look at how we use your Lights On and Lights Off signatures to activate your family's potential in a new way. This is when the Lights On metric guides you into a completely different paradigm. One where you unlock your hidden potential, within the Lights Off state, and unleash your exponential potential within your Lights On state. You and your family are capable of achieving so much more than you have been led to believe by the old-school standardised system.

PART THREE
ACTIVATING YOUR POTENTIAL

8
Tracking Your Lights On Spectrum

From the moment my children entered the school system, I refused to listen to the old-school thinking – 'This is how we do things, Julia!' I trusted my intuition, led from my heart and got my head in alignment. I took intentional inspired action to flex the system every which way to safeguard my children's mental wellbeing and love for learning. I skilled up fast to enable myself, my children and ultimately thousands of others to become outstanding learners. Along the way, I discovered that the thing that makes the biggest difference to a child's attitude, passion and aptitude for learning was not the work I or any other educator would do with them, but the mindset of their parents or primary carers. Do they view the world largely through a Lights On or Lights Off lens? How do they show up as learners?

Without exception, parents who have transformed their families to love learning the Lights On way have understood one simple truth: Lights On Learning begins with them. Once this lands, they stop looking for old-school solutions to fix their child. They open up and create a life of abundance, happiness, fulfilment and purpose. This inner wealth enriches every area of their lives, as Nicky shares:

> 'Learning to live Lights On is transforming my life. Navigating the unknown. Walking through fear and uncertainty. Trusting the process. This work is deep. It can be challenging, uncomfortable and confronting at times, as beliefs and thought patterns reveal themselves. Yet it is also simple, energising and liberating.
>
> 'Looking back, I see just how far I've come. I began with the hope of overcoming patterns of poor mental health. I now know this as my reality. It is happening, and from here anything becomes possible. My aspirations are expanding.
>
> 'I've found an inner freedom I couldn't imagine possible before. I'm reconnecting with my passions and stepping into who I was born to be.
>
> 'The effects of Lights On are rippling out to my family and now I lead them on a new adventure – empowering my children to

embrace a life of possibility, no matter what. An exciting journey ahead and one that I trust in completely.'

I love Nicky's powerful reflection. It shows how possible it is to rewire past thinking when you dare to dream big and ask for what you want in life. Nicky's vision is for her children to know how to use the power of their hearts and minds to live a fulfilling life, doing something they love. She wants them to have intrinsic motivation to be able to flourish, regardless of what obstacles come their way. To achieve this, she understood she had to commit to that for herself first. As an ecologist, writer, award-winning photographer and gardener, she is passionate about changing our relationship with nature, especially in our gardens. She has reconnected with her natural talents and tuned back into curiosity, awe and wonder in a new way. She is using her photography, writing and voice, through her podcast 'Unearthing Wild Wonders',[36] to engage hearts and change minds. She has learned to play an inner game of success which involves a lightness of spirit, and an ease and flow. This is a common pathway for parents when they begin their Lights On Learning adventure. They re-engage their hearts, heads and hands and become inspiring creators again.

---

36 N Jenner, 'Unearthing Wild Wonders' (2024), https://open.spotify.com/show/6CdQWsInC736CaxG0RTcDH?si=9WOM-GOpQjKZAX2XnpBN0w

- They become artists.
- They become musicians.
- They become writers.
- They become makers.
- They start their own micro-businesses.
- They find jobs that they love.
- They self-publish books.
- They produce podcasts.
- They set visions well beyond their edges.
- They feel calm, connected and confident.
- They find peace.
- They choose freedom.
- They define their own victory conditions.

Quite simply, when a parent owns their vision to lead their child to love learning, they rediscover themselves again…

'Ah, there I am. I was here all along.'

From this authentic place, they feel safe to dive deep into their own potential to lead their family to explore and fully express all they can be. When you know how to live and learn in this way, your children will, too. Lights On Learning is about who we become as we step fully into who we were born to be: fully expressed, authentic creators.

So, are you ready for the next stage, where we activate your family's potential? It begins with using your unique Lights On spectrum as a self-awareness and calibration tool to track your internal state, upgrade your learning circuits and grow in a new way.

Customise your Lights On spectrum

You've already got clarity on your Lights Off and Lights On signatures from the previous two chapters. Bring these together so you have the blueprint of your entire Lights On spectrum, from Darkness to Radiance.

Here's an example from Katrin:

My Lights On spectrum
- When I feel Lights Off and Lights On, what thoughts and feelings do I have?
- What emotions do I experience?
- What sensations do I feel and where do I feel them in my body?

LIGHTS ON LEARNING

Lights On/Off signatures	Thoughts and feelings	Emotions	Where I feel it in my body
Radiance	Wow! This is working out better than I could have imagined.	Gratitude, joy, peace	Warmth in my chest, smile on my face
Brilliance	This is exciting. I love being me.	Love, contentment	Softness in my whole body
Glow	I can do this. I am safe to try.	Optimism, inspiration	Grounded in my feet, connected to the earth
Glimmer	I wonder what this would look like.	Uncertainty, curiosity	Tingling in my chest
Dimness	I can't do this. I have nothing to offer.	Anxiety, fear, frustration	Tight throat, teary eyes
Darkness	This is not safe. I can't move forward.	Judgement, hopelessness	Sick in the stomach

↑

Start here!

If you are still unsure of some of your Lights On and Lights Off signatures, remember this is an ongoing process, full of nuance. There is no right or wrong. The key is to spark the conversations within your family, as Katrin shares:

'The Lights On spectrum has been hugely helpful to us as a family to explore the whole range of human emotions in a nonjudgemental way. Realising that true learning involves circling through the entire spectrum was a game changer in normalising emotions as part of our learning experiences. It also helped me as the leader of my family to shift from thinking that something needed "fixing", to helping my children to accept and move through their emotions in a constructive and empowering way. We now have a shared language and awareness guiding us to greater emotional intelligence as well as building emotional resilience whether we face failure or success.'

Getting your family on board

I've taken enough parents through my Lights On spectrum training to know a common Lights Off thought is 'My child (or teenager) won't agree to this.' However, if you don't ask you won't know, so be mindful of where your own thinking is limiting your child's access to this incredible learning tool. Take Karen's ten-year-old son, for example, who created his own scale of cool. 'My son embraced it and made sense of it in a way I had not anticipated,' she explains. 'I got him to calibrate his own spectrum and he did this with joy and ease. I loved the way he made sense of this in an instant and in his own words.'

I also love the way he made this his own. When in Darkness, his thoughts were, 'I'm not cool. I don't like who I am.' In Radiance, his thoughts were, 'I'm flippin' cool.' I love his description in Glimmer: 'Maybe I'm cool.' His main feeling was 'curiosity (but not the kind that killed the cat), the tiniest cheese slice of hope'. And in Glow, 'I'm cool' with the emotion of 'feeling rad, like on a bicycle downhill (in a good way)'.

When children use the Lights On tools, they access it in a way that makes intuitive sense to them. It doesn't have to be big and heavy, as we can so often make it. My son, aged seventeen when I first shared my Lights On spectrum with him, particularly liked how it normalised being Lights Off. I thought this was insightful. More open conversations in our families around having a fluid and dynamic movement through the Lights On spectrum is beneficial to our mental, emotional and physical health.

Begin tracking

It's time to collect your first round of data by tracking your Lights On and Lights Off status three times a day over two weeks. This will give you fresh insights into how your Lights On and Lights Off signatures affect how you lead yourself through life. Your thoughts, feelings and emotions will influence your rhythm and flow of learning, creative energy, self-expression and achievements. The data makes it clear where you are being intentional and visionary about your success, or where you are being reactionary.

Step one: Capture your data

Set yourself up for success by creating a system for collating your data that works for you. You can make a simple spreadsheet, draw a table in your journal or get creative.

For example, Sarah chose to create a visual diary of her internal journey by taking photos of herself with different facial expressions. She edited them together with fun sound effects and it captured the energetic tone of her week, revealing how fluid and dynamic her internal state was. She also tried recording it on paper, which looked like an energetic pulse over time.

Nicky and her family chose to create an emotions colour wheel and pin it on the fridge so her young children could access it easily. Rachel embraced the spreadsheet and played around with Google Forms to make the data entry easier for her family. Kayte knew she wanted her teenagers involved so created a family WhatsApp tracking group where she sent a daily poll. I tried this with my two and it worked well. The best way to make this successful is to explore and experiment to find what works best for you. Just don't overcomplicate it!

Step two: Set yourself up for success

Set a reminder on your phone for morning, afternoon and evening. Label it 'Lights On status'. Without this reminder, you may not remember and then become demotivated. You don't want to leave any room for excuses. 'Oh, I forgot. I'll do it tomorrow.' Success for this task is binary:

- Did you set an alert? Yes/No
- When it went off, did you check in with your Lights On status? Yes/No
- Did you record it? Yes/No
- Did you do it daily for two weeks? Yes/No
- Did you use your data to reflect and gain insights about your internal state of being? Yes/No

Step three: Get curious

When your reminder goes off, ask yourself, 'Where am I on the Lights On spectrum right now?' When your answer or insight lands, record your data. Notice if there is any resistance to declaring which signature you are in. When I started tracking, I noticed that I sometimes wanted to put higher ones to make myself feel better. As soon as that thought popped into my head, I put the next signature down. If I had a doubt, then I chose to track at a lower level so that I didn't fall into the trap of 'fooling myself' that I was more Lights On than I was. This is particularly important with the comfort zone gradients of Glow and Glimmer, where it can easily go either way.

Step four: Add context

Write down specific thoughts and emotions and explore how this signature either serves or hinders you, in this moment. If you are in the Lights Off gradients, what thoughts need your attention and what would move you up the spectrum? If you are in the high levels of Lights On, then take a moment to anchor in the feelings to sustain this elevated state. Bottle up the essence, so you can attune to it at a later date. Sarah asked herself questions like, 'What colour or image is each signature?' to anchor her insights into how she thinks and learns best.

Step five: Celebrate

Once you've entered your data, celebrate your micro-win of taking intentional action. Even celebrating three times a day is going to change your life by itself. Your learning circuitry will love it and may even lift you a signature or two as you track through the two weeks.

LIGHTS ON LEARNING

Intentional daily check-in

At the end of every day, take a moment to check in and reflect in your journal:

- How did my thoughts, emotions and feelings serve me today?
- What intentional action did I take to ascend, or sustain myself, at a particular signature?
- If I became stuck in a Lights Off signature, what thoughts kept me there? If I cascaded rapidly down into the lower Lights Off signatures, what was the trigger? Was it external, such as something someone said or did? Or was the trigger internal, maybe I was hungry and didn't notice the signals before I became hangry?!

Your answers to these questions will increase your self-awareness, and you will become more conscious and intentional about being Lights On or Off. Remember, you get to choose.

Three-day check-in

Three days into your Lights On tracking, you will spot emerging patterns. Are you staying stuck in Darkness or Dimness? Does Radiance seem unavailable to you? Use these questions as prompts:

- Am I experiencing the full range of the Lights On spectrum or am I staying in one or two particular signatures?

- How does my Lights On state correlate with other family members? Do I find myself shifting to someone else's signature? If so, is there one person in particular that affects my internal state more than others?

- Is there a trend around the time of day or particular activity where I seem to find myself in the Lights Off signatures?

- If I, or any family member, have been in Darkness – how long did we stay there?

- Were we able to shift into Dimness or did we become stuck in Darkness?

- Did I/they feel able to ask for help?

For now, simply be curious about the emerging trend. Look at the insights you gained and wonder how you would like your pattern to shift. Maybe you are comfortably hanging out in Glow and Glimmer but would like to access Brilliance and Radiance more intentionally. Perhaps you are triggered constantly into Dimness or Darkness and you want to stop that roller coaster that cascades you to an emotional low.

Your blueprint baseline

Repeat this trend-spotting on days seven and twelve to become more conscious of how your Lights On and Lights Off states affect the choices you make, the actions you take and your experience of life.

Charlotte realised this after a two-week round of tracking:

> 'I have been much more aware of my thoughts, assumptions and narrative that I tell myself. It's been less "I'm feeling down" or "I'm feeling motivated", but more drilling down into what's making me feel that way and trying to make an active decision to change my thinking. I feel I'm still in the early stages of rewiring but I will persevere.'

The first round of tracking can be confronting, especially if your baseline is mainly in the Lights Off signatures. Many parents discover they have been living comfortably between Glimmer and Glow, and when it fully lands that they have a choice in what they think, feel and how they act, they find it empowering. As Allison discovered after her first two weeks of tracking: 'The awareness that you're in the driving seat is liberating and uplifting.'

Glow or below

It is easy to become stuck in Glow and Glimmer as this is a cosy place to be. Not too dark, but not too bright either. When Glow is the brightest you shine, it feels great compared to being Lights Off. You feel expansive and safe to dream and can fall into the trap of wishful thinking and daydreaming. Instead of taking action, you bathe in the imagined possibilities and promises of what is to come. You get the feel-good factor from the visioning process itself and feel as if you already have it, but you can lose motivation to take action to get there. You know, in your heart and gut, that there is more you could achieve, but you simply don't know how to access the peace and freedom that is waiting for you in Radiance. This leads to a growing sense of being unfulfilled because you are not accessing the multiple growth spirals available to you. You're not seeing your growth, which is what is so rewarding with Lights On Learning, what you can achieve seems limitless. Look out for whether Glow has become your glass ceiling, as Nicole shares:

> 'I sat very comfortably in Glow – feeling life was great. As I used meditation to ascend the spectrum, I found a lot of resistance and discomfort being in Brilliance. It somehow didn't feel safe and my life would somehow crumble if I stayed there or moved to Radiance. The thoughts and feelings would

creep in that would keep me there "just in case it went wrong"! I now trust that "it" won't go wrong and that being in Brilliance and Radiance is even better for productivity, creativity and connection.'

The Lights On spectrum is a calibration tool

Using your Lights On spectrum as a self-awareness tool can lead you to a more balanced, resilient and vibrant sense of self. When you use it intentionally to align your thoughts, emotions and actions with your vision, it becomes powerful.

Are your thoughts working against you because you are in a Lights Off signature?

> I can't do this, it's too hard + Resignation, Defeat + Procrastination = Stuck

Or can you get your thoughts to work for you by accessing a Lights On signature?

> I've got this + Inspired, Optimistic + Writing daily = A published book!

Sarah's lightbulb moments clearly show how she uses the Lights On spectrum to align her thoughts with her vision to make taking action inevitable:

'In my version of me that is fulfilling my family vision, I keep promises and commitments and I am true to my word. I have clarity about what course of action to take or decisions to make at any one moment.

'This is different from the familiar keep-myself-safe strategy (belief) of "not knowing what is the right decision/course of action" and therefore delaying decision making or changing my mind (action).

'What's landed in a new way, is the bridge between the two. When I am aligned with my intentions, then commitment is not a problem and making promises is a choice made with certainty.

'The second lightbulb moment is feeling the difference between outside-in and inside-out thinking. Acting on my vision only when I see evidence from the outside is a familiar roller coaster of enthusiasm followed by disappointment. Acting on my vision from an inner knowing/inner Radiance, a belief that is precious and living within me, and a certainty that (a commitment that) all is well, whatever things look like from the outside, brings the clarity and confidence I seek.

'At once I can relax into being me and enjoying life and cease the endless pursuit of pleasing others and trying to get it right before I move forward.'

LIGHTS ON LEARNING

So powerful. Being in tune with your Lights Off and Lights On signatures is what makes Lights On Learning different from the old-school model of education. In the next chapter, we'll take another step to receive the Lights Off thoughts that come knocking at your door, inviting you to grow with compassion and look at how to rewire your learning circuitry. Lights On Learning is not a 'smile and think positive thoughts' strategy. It is an internal rewiring job so that your family can develop a next-level learning circuitry and be Lights On more often, for longer periods. Time to align your thoughts, emotions and actions with your vision, because to have a family that loves learning and is happy, engaged and self-led requires action. However, we want that to feel simple for you to take.

9
Rewiring Your Lights Off Circuitry

In October 2016, I crashed and burned. I hit rock bottom on my entrepreneurial emotional roller coaster. I was now a single mum of a ten-year-old and a thirteen-year-old, working on overdrive to keep my business going.

At this stage, I was still operating in the old-school 'outside-in' success model of 'pushing on through'. In many ways, I enjoyed the thrill of the highs and lows and solving the multitude of problems I faced. I prided myself on being a problem-solver, who could come up with solutions to anything. I thought the emotional high of feeling invincible one moment followed by the low of feeling hugely vulnerable was how things were for entrepreneurs. It was the price you paid for having a big vision. Or so I believed.

As my mission needed more from me and my team, things began to unravel fast. One of my mentors decided to leave and recommit to her own business. Another wanted to work fewer hours. Just a few weeks into opening a second centre, on a school site, another handed in her notice, effective immediately. The moment I received her email, something in me shut down. I disconnected. Like a switch turning off. I felt an overwhelming sense of wanting to quit, too. It seemed so unfair that my team could come and go but I had to keep going, regardless of whether I felt I could or not. I wanted to close up shop and run away. To be free of the entrepreneurial Groundhog Day I felt stuck in and not have to unpick the old-school thinking in new team members. I was done with holding space for their mistakes while they grew into the role. I'd had enough. I wanted out of my vision. I had nothing left to give.

I returned to my mum's, and for four days I pretty much stayed in bed and cried. It still feels raw to think about that time. I wanted nothing to do with the world around me. My mum and sister were concerned as it was so out of character. I was strong, formidable, even, but here I was curled up and defeated. I had failed massively and reached the end of the road. I felt completely directionless like my inner navigational system had shut down. Completely Lights Off. I didn't care about anything I was so deep in my emotional suffering.

Truth was, I later discovered, I had exhausted my ability to outperform my subconscious mind. My Lights

Off thought, 'I can't do this, it's too hard', that I'd hardwired in during my adventurous childhood, was getting overwhelming evidence that, after all this persistence, I couldn't do it. All I could think was, what now? I had been searching for my purpose all my life and thought I'd found it. If I let go now, I would have to begin again, age forty-seven. I felt backed into a corner, in complete Darkness. Depleted of energy. Mentally exhausted. Emotionally drained.

On the fourth day, my sister, who trained in suicide prevention for her humanitarian work, asked me about my state of mind.

'Julia, can you see a way forward? How concerned do we need to be?'

Her direct questioning flicked my lights back on, momentarily.

'I don't have a choice,' I said.

'You do have a choice.'

'Yes, I do have a choice,' I realised.

This was not how my story would end: that I never realised my vision for a more egalitarian education system because it was 'too darn hard' so I gave up. I would find a way. I would 'persist, persist, persist', but in a new way. The success path I was desperately clinging on to was not sustainable anymore, or enjoyable. It was impacting my family and damaging my mental health. I decided to keep my centres open for one more academic year to put my philosophy and approach to the test and go online to reach as many families as I could. In my search for personal growth and to stay committed to my vision, I discovered the ability to rewire my brain. Using the power of our minds and our brains' neuroplasticity, it turns out we have pretty superhuman powers most of us never use.

Shining a spotlight on your most limiting beliefs

Your brain's ability to prune away old neural networks and wire in new ones is key to learning, growth and mastery. Most of your Lights Off circuitry has been hardwired during childhood when your brain's plasticity is turned right up. Your early experiences, in your family, school and community influence how you make sense of, and react to, the world around you, throughout your life. How you think, feel and behave determines whether you stay safe, loved, valued and that you belong. This also sets the tone for who you are as a learner.

If you grew up in a predominantly Lights Off environment, it might feel too risky to tune into Brilliance or Radiance. 'Who do you think you are? You've got ideas above your station. Don't put your head above the parapet.' Equally, if your family was very Lights On, then showing any moments of doubt, sadness or desperation might have been glossed over with positivity and optimism. 'What've you got to be sad about? Come on, buckle up. Be strong. Everything is going to be fine.'

Whatever you're discovering about your baseline Lights On status, one thing is certain: you will benefit from consciously flushing out your Lights Off circuits by tuning into your inner self-talk every day.

Set up a daily discipline of metacognition

I think of the power of metacognition – thinking about thinking – as a growth tool. When I first heard my subconscious thoughts loud and clear, it was life-changing. From that moment on, I was on a path to freedom, achieving a sense of peace, even when in Darkness, that I hadn't even known was possible. Tune in with anticipation to how your life is going to change when you can use your Lights Off thoughts to work for you, rather than hold you back.

I suggest you set an alert on your phone, five times throughout the day, and label it: 'What am I thinking?' It might feel strange at first, and you might find yourself thinking, 'I don't know what I'm thinking.' Simply note that down! The more you commit to this intentional act of catching your thoughts, the quicker you will become self-aware.

If you are more of a feeler than a thinker, you may experience the emotion in your body first. If this is the case, you might want to use the question 'What I am feeling?' and put words to the sensations you are experiencing, and then ask the follow-up question: 'What are my thoughts behind this feeling?'

The situation is neutral

One of the first things I learned when training as a Master Neurocoach, is that the situation is neutral. When you work with groups of children, you see this clearly, as children will experience situations in entirely different ways. It is important, therefore, to practise neutralising the charge of any situational trigger because you can't change what happened. What you can change is your mental and emotional reaction to it.

Take Claire for example. Every morning, her son would eat his porridge and leave the empty bowl on the table. Claire would see the porridge bowl and her Lights Off circuitry would be immediately triggered. Getting angry, she would snap, 'Why can't you just put that bowl away?' This, of course, triggered a negative response from her son. Her thoughts were: 'He never puts his bowl away. He is so lazy. My kids never do anything for me. They don't care about me. What am I, a servant?' When she learned to neutralise the situation and saw it as 'an empty porridge bowl', she was able to let go of the emotional charge around it. What happened was incredible. Without her having to even ask, her son started putting it in the dishwasher! I like to think the porridge bowl had served its purpose in bringing some Lights Off circuits to Claire's attention. What's your equivalent of Claire's porridge bowl?

Rewiring your circuitry

Think of a situation with your child that always triggers you. Then use my WIRE framework to use your situational trigger for growth. Remember, the situation is neutral, so keep any 'storytelling' or narrative out, and limited to what others can observe – for example, an empty bowl left on a table by a child.

W – Witness The Flicker

I – Identify The Short Circuit

R – Reframe For Radiance

E – Energise The Circuit

W – Witness The Flicker

As soon as your internal light starts to dim, try to notice the energetic shift in your body and get curious about what Lights Off signature you've shifted into. Remind yourself that the situation itself is neutral and focus instead on the factual details. For instance, 'I'm in Darkness, feeling scared and unsafe. I feel sick in my stomach and my legs feel shaky.' Then allow your emotional response to play out. According to Dr Jill Bolte Taylor's research, it takes about ninety seconds for the chemical process created by an emotion to pass through your body.[37] Use this time to sit and observe yourself experiencing the emotion. This will stop you from spiralling into a negative thought-feel loop, where your thoughts fuel your emotions, which in turn supercharge your thoughts.

I – Identify The Short Circuit

Highlight your Lights Off thought patterns by asking yourself, 'What was I thinking just before I felt the shift into Lights Off?' Let your thoughts flow naturally, don't censor them. Get your main Lights Off thought and how it makes you feel out of your head and onto paper. This will interrupt the negative self-rumination and see it for what it is, an outdated thought pattern. You may find your thoughts become childlike as you expose the old wiring and get to the source belief, which is essentially a thought and emotion repeated frequently that has become hardwired in as an automated neural network. You'll feel a sense of recognition, relief and 'yep, that's it', and you might also feel some big emotions, such as anger, sadness or grief. With self-compassion, if you feel safe to do so, try to go a level deeper to uncover the entanglement of

---

37 WUSA9, 'The 90 second life cycle of an emotion' (2021), www.youtube.com/watch?v=vxARXvljKBA, accessed 25 August 2024

thoughts and emotions that have created your Lights Off circuitry. What is it you are thinking when you get to the source belief?

R – Reframe For Radiance

Next, you want to cross-examine your Lights Off thought and expose it as a lie. I like to use Byron Katie's inquiry question, 'Is it true?' with the addition of, 'In all cases and scenarios?'[38] Is this true, in all cases and scenarios? If you find yourself advocating for the thought, you probably haven't gone deep enough to get to the source of the thought that feels exposing, such as when I uncovered the thought 'I'm not loveable'. You only need one bit of evidence to expose it as a lie, so find it. Write down one logical reason why this thought is not true. 'My kids love me, so it's not true. I am loveable.' If possible, think of another. 'My sister loves me. My mum loves me. My dad loved me. My dog absolutely loves me!' And another. 'I love me.'

Note that this is not just about immediately reversing your thoughts into a positive. You need to defuse the emotional charge so that when someone says to you, 'Who do you think you are, you love yourself don't you?', you can say, 'Yep, I really do.' Neutral. Fact. I love being me!

---

38   B Katie and S Mitchell, *Loving What Is* (Random House, 2008)

To defuse the emotional charge, you can imagine someone you'd consider a bully saying your Lights Off belief to your younger self, to your child or someone vulnerable. 'You're not loveable. Look at you. Who would love you? You're worthless.' You want to feel the urge to stand up for yourself, or the person you are imagining, because you can see how painful this would be to hear this, over and over again, as you are doing to yourself. Painful, right? With such negative self-talk, no wonder you feel like you do in certain situations. It is normal to feel what you do, with that thought on a loop. Be an advocate for yourself and open up to your truth instead.

E – Energise The Circuit

With your Lights Off circuit identified, cross-examined and exposed as a lie, it is time to focus on the thoughts, emotions and beliefs you want to consciously hardwire in. You don't want to do a patch-repair job and just think positive thoughts as you'll still be reactive to situational triggers and be exhausted by constantly having to reframe. Instead, you want to fully prune away the Lights Off neural connections and hardwire in new Lights On circuitry. You can create a brain bridge to help you believe your new statement. For example, if you have flushed out the Lights Off belief that 'I am a rubbish leader', a positive affirmation would be 'I am an inspired leader'. You are not likely to believe it yet, as it's too big a stretch of the imagination. Instead, use 'I'm learning to become an inspired leader'. Now when you try to lead your family and it doesn't work, you can remind yourself, 'That's ok, I'm learning on the job,' rather than, 'I'm rubbish, I'm letting my family and myself down. I'll never help my son love learning.'

An example of the WIRE process

Situational trigger	My son left his empty porridge bowl on the table again. That's eight days in a row!
Lights Off thought(s)	He never puts his bowl away. He is so lazy. My kids never do anything for me. They don't care about me. What am I, a servant?
Lights Off feeling	Angry and frustrated. Tired. Fed up. Disrespected.
Source belief	I don't matter, nobody cares about me, I'm not valued.
Cross-examination	That's not true. My children tell me all the time how much they love me, and how I make them feel safe. I am also valued at work, and I know I contribute a lot of value to my team.
Defusing the emotional charge	'No one values you. I can't think of anything you bring into the mix. You might as well not exist.'
	That's not true, I value myself.
	My value is not attached to what I do.
	I am valued because of who I am.
New belief(s) to hardwire	I am valued for who I am, not for what I do. I am loved. I bring a lot of value to my family. I matter.

Prime in your Lights On circuit

When you have your Lights On thought, you want to supercharge it with Radiance by tuning into love and gratitude. We'll look at this in the next chapter. Record yourself saying your new belief and listen to it several times a day to speed up the automation of your new neural network – 'I'm learning to become an inspired leader. Oh yes, I am!'

If you take a leaf out of James Clear's *Atomic Habits* strategy, you can habit stack.[39] Hardwire in your new belief when you do an existing habit. For example, every time you turn on the kettle to make a cup of tea, tune into Radiance and say to yourself, 'I'm learning to become an inspired leader.' Take a deep breath and anchor it in with the anticipation of your child loving learning.

This will prune away your Lights Off neural network and hardwire in your new Lights On belief. This takes consistent, intentional effort over time and the more you think the thought, the faster it will automate. Set an alert on your phone and say it often, especially when you are feeling love, gratitude, peace and joy.

As with using all the Lights On Learning tools, it may take you a while for this to become second nature. Remember why you are doing this work: so your

---

39   J Clear, *Atomic Habits: An easy and proven way to build good habits and break bad ones* (Penguin Random House, 2018)

child can be happy and engaged and lead themselves to love learning. This will give you the motivation and courage to keep going. Now it's time to learn how to tune into Radiance on demand, so you no longer have to be dependent on circumstance to be Lights On. You have it hardwired in.

10
Opening Up To Radiance

It was eighteen years ago that I began my adventure to explore learning, growth and human potential. It feels surreal to see where I've arrived because, to begin with, there was no plan, not even a vision. Being an educator or neurocoach was not on my radar. Although slowing down to be present for my kids, I still very much identified as being a documentary maker. I can see now, however, that there were a series of clear actions and choices I made that led me here. One phone conversation, with a man from the Local Education Authority, stands out as pivotal to opening this portal. I want to give him a name, as he unknowingly changed my life. Let's call him Simon. To him, I was probably just another parent who was not happy with how their child was feeling in school.

I explained to Simon that my daughter had started school full-time. She was summer-born, and, just four years old, was struggling with the long days. Since going full-time, I had seen a change in her mood and a deterioration in her mental health. I felt it was too much and wanted to continue the part-time arrangement of the six-week staggered entry. Was that possible? I was fully expecting him to say no. To my surprise, he said yes: 'It's called flexischooling. You just have to get permission from the head teacher.'[40]

So that was what I did. Every Thursday, Esme stayed at home to learn with me and her younger brother, Seb. This sparked my commitment to play an active role in unlocking my children's learning potential throughout their educational careers. They are both phenomenal learners who understand that mental and emotional resilience isn't about being strong all the time or ignoring your Lights Off thoughts and emotions. It is about being vulnerable enough to shine your spotlight directly on the source of emotional discomfort and pain. It's also about being brave enough to tune into the life-enhancing power of Radiance.

Cracking your personal code

In Chapter 5, I presented the Lights On spectrum as an ascending spiral from Darkness up to Radiance. Your thoughts can either spiral you upwards or cascade

---

40   See Finding The Flex: www.findingtheflex.com/, accessed 11 Sep. 2024

you downwards, energetically. I now invite you to conceptualise your Lights On spectrum as a personal code for you to crack so you can use it to access your creative energy when you need it most, as Sarah's insight reveals:

> 'I'm struck by the difference between using the Lights On spectrum as a gauge of emotions and using it as a tool. If I'm using the spectrum to simply check my emotions, I might choose to stay there and not bother to ascend because there doesn't seem to be a point. However, if I make the spectrum relevant to that day, it becomes a tool based on asking the right question.'

For example, if you want to feel calm, content and happy, you can choose to access Glow. If you need to be in full creation mode, you may open up the energising signature of Brilliance. If you want a more grounded, serene connection, where you feel peace, you can clear the way for Radiance.

Radiance is the essence of who we are

As you activate your Lights On state more frequently, you'll discover Radiance isn't a pinnacle state to aim for, but an inherent part of your core being. It is where your true essence shines the brightest. I think of it as our renewable energy source, like the sun that always shines, regardless of the clouds that cover it up. You probably don't wake up in the morning and doubt the sun will rise. You trust it will. It's a belief you have. The sun rises and sets every day. Once you believe that Radiance is always available to shine through you daily, you'll have more faith in your ability to access it by choice. While your Lights Off thoughts, emotions and limiting beliefs may momentarily overshadow your inner light, your Radiance is always present, no matter how dark your thoughts and emotions become at times.

Let's remind ourselves of the powerful nature of Radiance with this insight from Jo:

> 'Radiance is not a state to be reached, it is a place to be found. It is in your inner core. Your true essence where you are being, not doing. It allows our unique identity to shine. When creating in Radiance, it is done with ease; from creating a masterpiece, solving a problem or preparing the family meal. The energy you bring to the situation makes the task feel like you are freewheeling down a hill with gravity doing all the work.

> 'Your mind is at peace, no judgement or doubt and you do not need external validation to keep going. There is a knowing you are in your purest form. Radiance cannot be hidden, you glow, radiating the energy to everyone you meet. The beauty at this level is that being self-conscious is not a thing so you are freely offering this to all you meet.

'Radiance is not an endpoint. Once discovered, you can return to it if you choose. Hold it gently as it is a springboard to new growth which will spiral you back to the Lights Off signatures on the spectrum. However, if you choose to take this challenge, you know that the new growth will enable Radiance to expand, unlocking the hidden potential that you carry inside.

'This is the lifelong journey exploring and realising your hidden potential knowing that living life in Radiance is going to be where your lifelong dreams can be realised. Wherever you are, Radiance is with you, and as you grow, Radiance will grow with you.'

I love this description, particularly because it marked a pivotal moment for Jo, where she reconnected with Radiance and took her own Lights On Learning to a new level.

Growth spirals

Connecting to your Radiance enables you to upgrade your learning circuitry and play the biggest game of your life. You become expansive in your thinking and find the courage to step beyond the edges of your comfort zone. 'If I can do that, then maybe I could do this?' As you head into the unknown and face a new level of uncertainty, you will inevitably find yourself being Lights Off again as a result. It is important to note, however, that you have not landed back at square one, but are in fact on a new growth spiral. This is like experiencing Lights Off, but from a new vantage point, where infinite possibilities open up to change your relationship with learning.

Confronting reality

There is no getting away from the fact that Darkness feels like a scary place to be. Life is hard, even brutal, at times. We don't gloss over that. Fear stops us in our tracks and cascades us into Darkness. Normalising being Lights Off, but intentionally doing the work to not stay there, has been pivotal for me, and so many parents in my community. Knowing how to make the energetic shift from Lights Off to Lights On is life-changing, as Ruth describes here:

> 'I've had a few experiences where I am feeling the intensity of being in Darkness or Dimness and it has led me to look at the thoughts fuelling those emotions. I've followed the neural network out of desperation, reaching the core thought and with tears flowing. I've drained the tank, so to speak, and allowed the emotions of Darkness to be heard and accepted, then looked at whether they are true. After some words of love and kindness to myself, I have then sprung up to Brilliance, sometimes

Radiance. Feeling lighter, looking at the world through a different lens where colours are brighter and where I have a feeling of freedom. I think it's the release of the emotion combined with wiring in a new belief of what is true that results in moving up the spectrum. It's like a new piece of a jigsaw can be added to the unfolding realisation of who I am.'

Acknowledging the challenges we face, both internal and external, builds the case even more for Lights On Learning. To continue with an education system that is holding children, parents and teachers back from expressing their potential doesn't make sense. Systematically dimming their lights and keeping them stumbling in the dark is inhumane. We are switching off the potential of whole communities unnecessarily, and we can see the consequences of the anger, frustration and resentment that builds as a result. Learning is the most natural thing in the world for us to do, it is not meant to feel like a life sentence for any of us.

I breathe. I live. I learn. I am.

To many, this may sound naïve, but once you've seen evidence of what children can do, and how much potential we are wasting, you can't unsee it. You can choose to ignore it and put your blinkers on, and stay in the old-school paradigm, but for Lights On families, the old educational pathway is no longer sustainable, healthy or desirable. It's certainly not a success model I want my children, or yours, to rely on.

Radiance is a lifeline

Since connecting with Radiance, my relationship with being Lights Off has changed. I no longer fear being there. It has surprised me that, despite how emotionally painful being in Darkness can be, it can also feel like a safe and familiar place. It is your family's connection with Radiance that will gift them a choice, freedom and sovereignty over their experience of life, to be able to cope, even when life throws you a devastating curveball, as Carolina's powerful story shows:

> 'This tale takes a dark turn… but at the end it shines. If you prefer not to delve further, understand that I find myself in a radiant place within the darkness. This is the narrative of my active investigation into the place where darkness originates within me, how it lingers and how I can exist in it while radiating light. It's about the world, my world, and the possibility that I might depart sooner than anticipated.
>
> 'About two months ago, I underwent surgery to remove lumps from my breast. This has been occurring more frequently and more intrusively than my doctor and I were willing to admit. He has been conservative, quiet, positive and supportive, but now I've initiated

treatment to prevent further development of my breast cancer. It's not my first encounter with cancer treatment, but it is the first time as a mother and as someone older. I realise the genuine possibility of my demise so I want to convey something meaningful to my children, something that will impact their lives. Mostly, I want to discover why I entered this world before departing from it. I revived my meditation practice. I sit, I breathe, I find myself. I can feel the love for myself as a human impermanent being, the infinite love for others around me, compassion, forgiveness and an immense quietness that accompanies peace. There, I also found fear. I found darkness. The darkness that pulls me away. I see that this darkness stems from a deep fear, and this time it's the fear of not being here. A strong attachment to thoughts accompanies it, and I let it linger. I now realise it's like an out-of-body experience – dwelling in the past, the future, right, left, back and forth, but not here – I bring myself to the moment, connecting at a profound level to the intangible essence of being here, of being in me.

'Then I am radiance! I envision myself as a star in a dark sky, as an incredible being. This is what I came for in this life – to shine! In the most mundane, quotidian and palpable way. This is what we all came for in this human life, to shine! I now understand that the circumstances are just another opportunity to do that, to be that. This is my legacy to my little one – we are radiant beings, and each of us holds the power to be that, to be present, to be ourselves to our fullest potential. After the news, I chose to live my life as I normally do, but now with much more character, fully committed to experiencing joy, regardless of how long it lasts.

'There are myriad thoughts, feelings, ups and downs, narratives and histories that I want to write and erase… but for now, I ride in a bubble of radiance that I discovered in my darkness because I can choose the way I think because I can rewire my own experience, even if it's not what I dreamed of.

28.06.2024

'It has been almost a year since I wrote this. So much has changed. I have aligned with myself, with the world and with the power of contracting and expanding time. I am present, strong and I want to shine. Moments of darkness are still frequent, but like a river stream, they pass away, leaving the sound of moving pebbles at the bottom as a reminder of their passing. Last Wednesday, I had a full-body PET and CT scan. As I lay in the scanner for two hours, I could feel it – I was certain that I was well. No cancer was found.

'I am here to stay just a little longer… the fear reminds me that I am alive.'

Wow, Carolina! So powerful. You are a woman who came here to shine. Despite a life so often shrouded in fear, Carolina has cracked her personal code to Radiance, even when Darkness descends in such an overwhelming way. She has understood that being Lights On is not about denying or bypassing the Lights Off state. Rather, it is about being aware when the Lights Off signatures are activated and then feeling gratitude for their signal and letting them go and rewiring them. As Carolina learns how to use the guiding light of her heart, so does her eight-year-old son, who in his own words shared, 'I'm tracking to anchor in my happiness.'

Time and time again, I've witnessed the transformation that spreads within a family when a parent learns to harness their human technology to work for them, rather than against them. It takes courage to reach the point Carolina has arrived at. It is not by keeping our lights on all the time that we grow, but by being prepared to go fully into the dark. This is where we can rewire our learning circuitry to access a new level of light.

Radiance – an immersion in gratitude

We've already explored the power of love but another emotion opens the gateway to Radiance: gratitude. Learning how to tune into gratitude has enabled me to develop a calmer and more compassionate inner strength. As a natural thinker, however, it didn't come easy to me. I didn't get how to 'open my heart to gratitude' as I was all in my head. At first, I understood gratitude purely as an intellectual exercise, writing in my journal each day three things I was grateful for in my life, within my family or the world around me. It made sense, so I did it, but it felt like just another thing on my ever-expanding, daily, personal growth checklist.

Daily gratitude practice ✓

I knew I was missing the point. There had to be more to it, which is when I discovered how to embody gratitude and once again my experience of my life changed dramatically. I no longer have a 'gratitude routine' because I tune in to it to access Radiance from my first thought of the day. It is now part of my daily life and I intentionally calibrate to Radiance as often as I can. It is like a fast track to expressing my creative energy, to be Lights On. To think it, feel it and be immersed in it.

Shining bright ✓

When I am tuned into the power of love and gratitude together, it is impossible for Lights Off thinking to get a look in.

Your inner-smile memories

The way I feel gratitude is by tuning into memories that make me smile inside and out. Remember my story of my nine-year-old son expressing how much he loved being him? At any moment, I can draw on this memory. Eight years later, it is still powerful. When I visualise his face lit up with self-love, I instantly feel a deep warmth in my heart. My inner smile creates an outer smile on my face and this opens me up to feel love and gratitude.

I'd like to guide you through a Lights On activation so you can see how Radiance can become available to you with practice. I have developed the practice with my eyes open so I can use this technique wherever I am, whatever I am doing, but you can have your eyes open or closed.

Activate your Lights On state

Read the following instructions and then give the activation a go.

To bring your awareness into your heart, think of a memory where you felt an overwhelming sense of love, joy and peace. Where everything felt it was exactly how life should be for you, in that micro-moment. A memory where you were fully present experiencing life, with no need for it to be different. It could be a memory from when you were a child, or maybe when you achieved something challenging. Maybe it is as simple as a beautiful sunset. Or it might be seeing your child lit up and immersed in the moment, with a smile on their face.

With this memory front of mind, take three deep, slow breaths to spread a warm glow across your chest. Feel present to the internal experience of feeling the emotions of love and gratitude that your memories stir in your body.

Allow your smile from within to become a gentle smile on your face. Stay immersed in this whole-body experience, basking in Radiance for as long as feels natural.

Take a deep breath and turn that dial right up to amplify your gratitude to another level. Imagine, feel or sense a warm glow from your heart radiating into the space around you. Hold it for as long as feels comfortable, and then bring your awareness back to your breath, to your heart and the present moment.

How did you get on? If I can learn to crack the code to access Radiance, so can you. It's transformative when you embody love and gratitude as a fast track to Radiance.

Create an inner-smile memory bank

Aim to have at least three inner-smile memories to access on demand. These memories don't have to be big or spectacular. If it makes you smile on the inside, then it counts.

Knowing how to feel gratitude throughout your body feels great, so try to do it daily, if even for just ninety seconds. Then you can begin to infuse gratitude throughout your Lights On spectrum, which over time raises your baseline resonance, as these mothers from my community share:

> 'It's helpful for me if I feel gratitude in the lower signatures too because I know they are teaching me something.' (Charlotte)

> 'Gratitude, I feel, can be found and expressed in smaller doses in the lower signatures, and then it flourishes and expands the further up the spectrum I go. It kindly serves as a vessel to help me move from one signature up to another!' (Beci)

Start tuning into gratitude and see how it changes your ability to connect with your core Radiance. Everything from that place requires less effort and more intentionality.

Future-proofing your family

When you and your family know how to attune to Radiance by choice, you become conscious creators. You may find yourself feeling supported by a sense of something bigger than yourself, and serendipity comes into play. It can feel like you are tuning into magic and you can begin to use your power to make a positive impact in the world around you. It is within this higher Lights On signature that you use the full power of your Lights On Learning circuitry, as your Heartset, Mindset and Skillset come together in perfect unison.

Learning how to transform your Lights Off reactive state into a growth opportunity will ensure you stand out from the crowd because you know how to tune into your full creative energy. You will have the flexibility of mind, emotional intelligence and the courage to fail forward towards success that Lights On Learning offers and will shine brightly in the era of the creative and collaborative economy. You will be more confident to work with others and don't need to prove you can do it all by yourself. You know the sum of your parts is greater than the whole, so when you play to your strengths and allow others to do the same, you will achieve extraordinary outcomes. In fact, I believe this so much we even have an equation for it!

(Ordinary Me + Ordinary You) × Opportunity
= Something extraordinary

If the challenge you faced was just about re-engaging your family with learning, that would be relatively straightforward. Part One of my book offers you that roadmap, to find out what they love to do more than anything else and design their learning around that. If this was enough on its own, you would have solved it by now. It is the ability to use your mental and emotional state to become Lights On entirely through choice, not circumstance, that results in your ability to learn, grow and truly flourish in your most authentic way. By taking ownership of your inner learning landscape, the obstacles that kept you stuck before no longer hold you back. You get to decide how much light to shine at any given moment. How does this look in practice? Let's find out in the next chapter, in which we get to see how Lights On Learning is never about what, how, when or where you learn, but all about who you are being as a learner.

11
Calibrating For Success

It was the end of 2017 when I realised I had been asking the wrong question all my life. 'What am I here to do?' That little nine-year-old me, talking with my dad and wandering around my garden asking, 'How will I make my impact?' set off on an adventure searching for meaning and purpose all around the world. For forty years!

Even in my meltdown, just a year earlier, I had still been thinking, 'If I don't do this, what will I do?' This exploration – 'to do what I've come here to do' – led to a fantastic adventure through life. It felt good, sometimes even great, when I connected to Brilliance, but I felt there was more. Always more. Never quite enough, feeling the constant rumblings of being in Glimmer and Glow, and at times the pull of discontentment through to Dimness. It was like I was never arriving at this pre-determined destination. Wherever that was.

I now know I was chasing the old-school, outside-in success criteria that came with other people's milestones and accolades. When I have X, I will be able to do Y, then I will be happy, fulfilled and purposeful. These were, and are, the wrong victory conditions for me, and I suspect they are for you, too.

Why am I here? Because I am

My quest is now focused on answering the question 'Who am I being?' This gets right to the core of leading myself, and my family, while aligned with my values. Tuning into my Lights On spectrum daily influences how I show up and opens up what I can, and do, achieve. It also massively changes who I can become. I am now aware that life presents us with the opportunity to experience a constant evolution of self. While I still feel there is more, always more, it is now through the magnetic pull of Radiance. It is an abundant quest for more, full of curiosity, awe and wonder. It is linked to me having the courage to take action beyond my edges. 'If I can do this, imagine what might be possible if I am brave enough to go one step further. What could I do if I set my heart, mind and skills to it?'

Courage, for me, is no longer about pushing through pain, fear or challenges with brute force and strong willpower. It is about being open to feeling it all. Lights On. Lights Off. The whole light spectrum. Every day, I am intentional about using my thoughts and emotions to align my actions with the outcomes I want to achieve.

> Thoughts + Emotions + Actions = Outcomes

Some days, I am more successful than others, as I suspect is true for you, too. However, something I am certain of is this…

When you shine, your family can, too

My book wouldn't be complete without introducing you to Rachel. A home-educating mother of three.

> 'I was all over the place and didn't have a clear education strategy. I had a big insecurity about what I was doing and an underlying fear that my education provision wasn't good enough. So I was a little bit lost and looking for a solution.'

Rachel fully intended to stay quietly in the background of my community. However, she realised the impact on her when other parents shared their vulnerabilities, struggles, wins and celebrations to engage their children. She thought if she was brave enough to be visible, to be seen and heard, maybe she could have the same effect. The moment she stepped into our Lights On Universe everything changed for her and her family. As Rachel claimed her right to be happy, fulfilled and Lights On, she reconnected with her creative energy and grew at an exponential rate:

> 'I spent the first decade of parenthood trying to change everyone else: if only they would do X… but Julia shifted my perspective. The only person I could change, really, was myself, and from there I could learn to lead my family. If my children were to learn to follow their passions and shine brightly in the world, I had to lead the way. What were my passions? I had no idea.'

While it can feel like we don't know what we love to do anymore, we can all find something that switches on our lights. As Rachel used art and writing to communicate with us all, I could see she was a magical storyteller, and I helped her see that, too. As she allowed herself to fully explore her natural gifts, and in particular her love for music, a new adventure opened up:

> 'I began making music. It felt good but also tinged with guilt. A little voice in my head whispered that self-indulgence was a bad thing. I had to remind myself that I was role-modelling passion-led learning. I soon saw the results.

> 'The creative freedom made me a better mum: calmer, kinder, lighter. The more fulfilled I felt, the less I wanted to control my children. I saw that a lot of the hoops I wanted them to jump through were to prove I was good enough, and had nothing whatsoever to do with their true paths or their education. When I felt "good enough" and the children felt less controlled and more trusted, the culture in our home shifted dramatically. I stopped thinking of my creative pursuits as frivolous. I came to see them as an essential life force.'

With her creative energy now being expressed regularly, she began to grow exponentially. She started projects to grow her confidence and self-belief to be seen, heard and valued for who she was. She set herself challenges that played to her strengths, extended her beyond her edges, and gave her endless opportunities for growth through being both Lights Off and Lights On.

> 'I set about writing and recording ten songs in a year, to share with the world, and I did it! I also used my creative energy to launch a business, with my fifteen-year-old daughter, making and selling eco-friendly bubble bath through our online shop. It was a project I had been procrastinating on for two and a half years. As I learned to lead myself, I led my

family in a new way, as a role model following her dreams, no matter what.'[41]

As parents like Rachel learn in a Lights On way, they notice a Lights On effect happening within their families. This refers to the transformative change that happens in others as you become Lights On. Scientifically, this is explained as brain-to-brain coupling or neural synchrony.[42] It is where the emotional state and brainwaves between two or more people synchronise. I like to think of it as creating a family rhythm-scape, with a harmonious ebb and flow of creative energy, where you learn, grow and flourish together. This is what makes Lights On Learning so powerful and exciting as an educational blueprint – it enables whole families to transform and live their most happy, fulfilled and engaged lives. By empowering you, as the adult around your child, to heal, learn and grow in a new way, you light up your family's learning circuitry in a spectacular way. This moves you from being a dreamer into an explorer, creator and changemaker, as Rachel and so many parents I've worked with have done:

'When you find that thing that motivates you from the heart – that's the game changer.

---

41 Rachel's online shop can be found at https://rachelrose.co.uk/
42 Y Endevelt-Shapira and R Feldman, 'Mother–infant brain-to-brain synchrony patterns reflect caregiving profiles', *Biology*, 12/2 (2023), 284, doi: 10.3390/biology12020284; L Denworth, 'Brainwaves synchronize when people interact', *Scientific American* (1 July 2023), www.scientificamerican.com/article/brain-waves-synchronize-when-people-interact/, accessed 17 September 2024

Looking back, I was so concerned with old-school "shoulds" that I only remember my children having too much screen time and a sense of apathy. I was missing where their brilliance naturally shone out. Now, I have an artist refining her style, a dancer training daily and an engineer developing his Lego wizardry. Self-led learners. I'm so proud of them – of me, of us – as a family.'

I am so proud of Rachel, too, and all the children and parents I've worked with over the past two decades. When they understand learning in this way, they open up to this beautiful, rhythmic and dynamic dance through their personal Lights On spectrum. It is this fluid movement between Lights On and Lights Off that creates opportunities for their exploration, learning and growth on such an exponential level. A Lights On Learner, whatever their age, is capable of extraordinary learning. It is like all the limits placed on them in the old-school paradigm dissolve away and anything becomes possible.

Meet Bryony…

From fearful to unstoppable writer in less than six months

Just before lockdown in 2020, six-year-old Bryony started feeling scared and anxious about going to school. She complained of tummy aches and did everything she could to delay or avoid going in. When schools closed during the pandemic, her mother Nicky joined my community and we quickly discovered Bryony was anxious about handwriting. Her Lights Off self-talk was telling her she was 'rubbish at writing'. The more she avoided writing, the less she developed as a writer, and the old-school metrics highlighted her lack of progress.

Her mother already had a strong mindset and great leadership skills, so our focus was on using my LEARN model to create a growth spiral and get Bryony's lights back on so she could reconnect with learning. We took the pressure off learning to write and started with her Heartset – as we always do.

Step one: L – Light up your learning circuitry and engage your Heartset

This step is all about harnessing the potential of your Lights On states using your natural-born talents, strengths and curiosities. What was it that switched Bryony's lights on with ease? She loved drawing and learning and sharing facts about dinosaurs so we gave her time to explore, play and create with her toy dinosaurs. She spent time reading her books and had lots of conversations about what she was learning.

Step two: E – Explore, get wired for learning and grow your Mindset

Nicky built in some fun challenges as a family to create a strong, mistake-friendly culture. Then, when she thought it was time to try some writing, she asked Bryony if she felt ready. She did. We gave her a choice to give her agency and personal power. Did she want to write as much as she could in ten minutes, as they did in school, or take the time pressure off and write ten words? She chose to write ten words, with no time limit.

Step three: A – Activate your potential and build your Skillset

This step is all about aligning your Heartset, Mindset and Skillset with the sweet spot of learning. It is where a parent's role as a leader is crucial, and often where they stumble. The exploration part is simple, but they struggle with holding compassionate space for both Lights On and Lights Off signatures to come into play. This is where the gap between what our hearts want to express and our ability to deliver is exposed, and we can feel frustrated, disheartened or even angry. As they sat down to write, it was hard for Nicky to see her daughter so anxious, but she held space for them both to feel their Lights Off signatures. When Bryony reached six words, she wanted to give up. There were tears. Frustration. Panic. All a natural stress response to believing she couldn't do it. Nicky enabled her daughter to feel it all and feel safe to make that important shift from Lights Off – 'I can't!' – to Lights On – 'I can!'

When she became stuck at six words, Nicky asked, 'How many do you want to write?' Bryony responded, 'Seven, no eight, maybe nine', and then finished her sentence.

Amazing! Bryony did it. She wrote ten words! They celebrated big time. Nicky had led her daughter to turn distress into eustress, using the creative energy of her Heartset to grow her Mindset. Now it was time to develop her Skillset, which they did with a creative brief to make a homemade illustrated book with drawings and key characteristics written about her favourite dinosaurs. Once Bryony had taken ownership of her writing, she chose how and where she wrote her ten words a day to create her book.

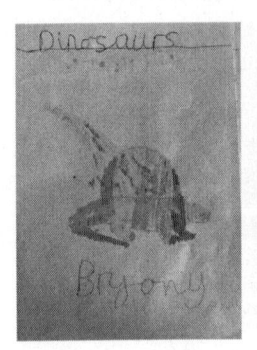

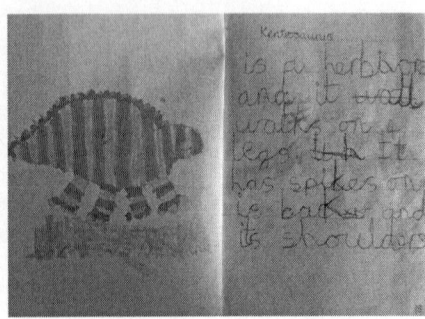

CALIBRATING FOR SUCCESS

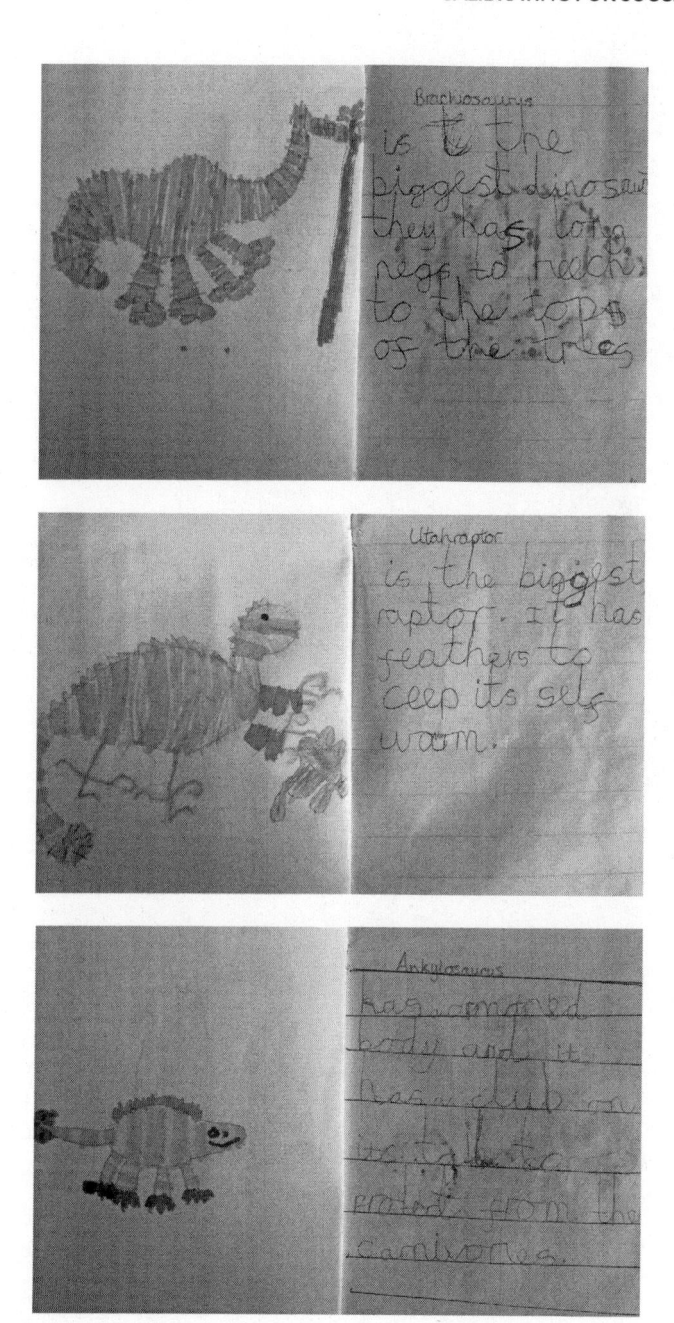

Brachiosaurus is the biggest dinosaur they has a long neck to reach to the tops of the trees

Utahraptor is the biggest raptor. It has feathers to ceep its self warm.

Ankylosaurus has armored body and it has a club on its tail to protect from the carnivores.

LIGHTS ON LEARNING

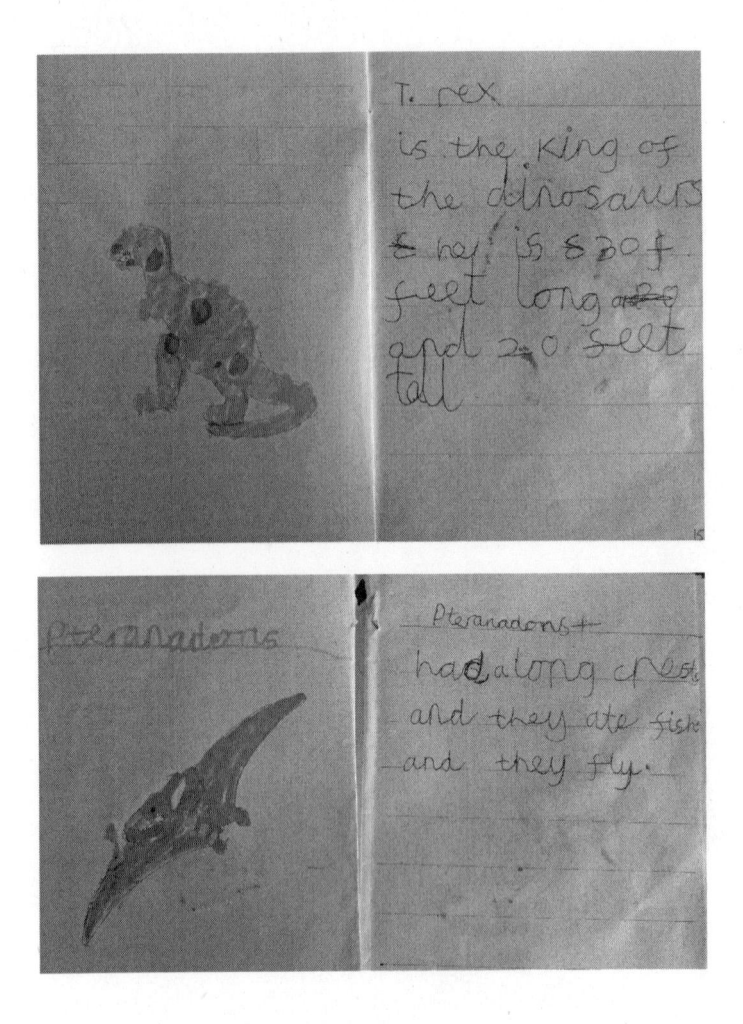

Step four: R – Reflect, review, rewire

This step is where we rewire the Lights Off neural circuits into Lights On ones and compound your success and open up possibilities. Nicky's leadership of

Bryony was phenomenal. She had led her daughter through massive fear and anxiety to be willing to put in the effort to get better. She helped Bryony see an alternative to her internal dialogue and gifted her the opportunity to move from 'I can't' to 'I can'. From Darkness to Radiance. From Lights Off to Lights On. By having evidence she could do hard things, overcome difficulties and keep on going, she had a new belief about herself. She can use her Lights Off moments to achieve hard things. Now it was time to develop her Skillset with more practice and repetition to hardwire the neurocircuitry that automates her handwriting skill.

Step five: N – New growth spiral and vision blueprint

Bryony was now in the driving seat of her learning adventure and, with evidence, she could grow through obstacles. This final step is about taking full ownership and setting goals for next-level growth. She wanted to write neatly like her best friend… and so she did. This is her writing just four months later. Lights On!

LIGHTS ON LEARNING

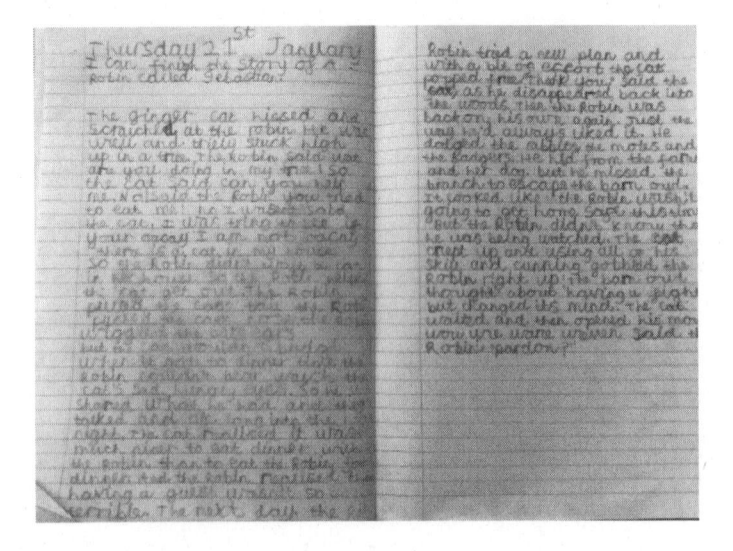

Wow! As is always the case, Bryony's teacher noticed the huge difference in her attitude and participation in the classroom. With her Heartset engaged, she could dream big, ensuring her Mindset and Skillset enabled her to adventure through her own Lights On spectrum. Nicky had helped her daughter believe she could achieve whatever she set her heart, mind and skills to. Happy, engaged and self-led.

Take a moment to imagine (think and feel) how Lights On Learning could change the way your child or whole family learns. How might things be different if you all knew how to use your Lights Off signatures for growth and your Lights On signatures for inspired creation? Tune into that vision of being a family that loves learning because if it is possible for all the families who have shared their stories and insights, it is possible for you, too.

Conclusion

Lights On Learning is an inner game anyone can play

At the core of the Lights On Learning philosophy and practical approach is the belief that success is an inner game. As humans, we perform best when we are fully connected with our creative energy through our emotional, mental, physical and spiritual connection. When our heart, head and body are fully engaged in the learning process, we instinctively know how to master our personal power. This is when we feel the freedom to learn, grow and flourish throughout our lives, regardless of the limitations of the environment we find ourselves in. As Viv so brilliantly put it, 'It feels like a remembering of who I am. A return to me.' This is exactly what it is.

We come into this world primed to love, connect and explore, and to be safe and survive, we need fear close by and accessible at all times. These seemingly conflicting ideas can either be two opposite sides, or polar extremes, as most of us experience them. Or they can be interconnected, as Carolina powerfully shared, offering us so much richness within our experience of being human. When you realise that your potential to shine is always within you, you have the power of choice. Just as you can choose to switch on the lights as you walk into a room, the same is true for you. You can be Lights On or Lights Off through conscious choice. The more your family attunes to what switches their lights on and what turns them off, the more they can activate and access their hidden and exponential potential.

In the old-school paradigm, it is common for children to come out of the entire fourteen years of education with nothing to show for themselves. Even if they ace the grades, they have little that sets them apart from the millions of A-graders around the world. Their true potential can go entirely unexplored and unexpressed for a lifetime. What a waste of time, energy and potential. It's like being in your home with all these fancy lights, and having the dimmer switch turned down to the lowest levels. You can't fully see what is in front of you because the light doesn't radiate out far. With Lights On Learning, that can never happen, because you get immediate, visible results.

CONCLUSION

We have made our children's disengagement a problem within our homes, schools and communities – 'Why is my child so unhappy and refusing to go to school?' Because it switches off their lights. They don't feel safe to express themselves. They feel like a failure. It makes them anxious. They find it draining. The list goes on. There are so many reasons why. Simple. No need for any complication or drama. By calling it a problem, we prop up a multibillion-dollar industry that offers old-school solutions and we, as adults (parents, teachers, health and mental health professionals), can avoid doing the inner work ourselves. We shine the spotlight on our children's behaviour, mental ill-health or neurodiversity and jump on the old-school narrative that the education system is broken. Maybe it is, but what if it isn't? What if by using the Lights On spectrum, we can gather meaningful data about whether a child's response is normal, healthy and appropriate to their thinking about the situation? Or we can identify where deeper underlying concerns are creating chronic or toxic stress, as a result of adverse childhood experiences (ACEs), such as household challenges, abuse or neglect.[43]

If a child gets stuck in Darkness for even a few days and you can't help them ascend to Glimmer or above, then I would encourage parents to seek professional help for some early intervention. However, learning

---

43 Centre on the Developing Child, *ACEs and Toxic Stress: Frequently asked questions* (Harvard University, 2019), https://developingchild.harvard.edu/resources/aces-and-toxic-stress-frequently-asked-questions/, accessed 22 August 2024

is as natural to us as breathing, so when we disconnect our children from learning, it is like starving their souls of oxygen. If our children couldn't physically breathe, we'd take them to the hospital straight away, like I did with my son's asthma attack after the circus. We need to take their mental health as seriously, as it is woven into their ability to learn, grow and flourish. As I've shared throughout, the solution begins with you.

I aimed to show you how simple this shift into a new paradigm can be, and for you to feel confident to jump on board a success path that aligns with your heart. We are at a crucial moment in the history of education evolution, because we are clearer than ever how we can use our hearts, heads and bodies to learn at phenomenal levels. With AI now in the mix, there has never been a more important time for us all to understand how to harness the full power of our human intelligence. I hope you believe that change is possible for your family because when you, as a parent, know how to flourish and live a life of freedom following your passions, with purpose, your family will have a whole new educational blueprint open up to them. This is when their lifelong adventure as learners can begin at a whole new level, leading them to be both Lights Off and Lights On.

A child, like all those you've met through this book, who disconnects from learning, for whatever reason, feels lost, scared and alone. We know this because when we ask they tell us. However, we also know because we see it in their eyes. They lose their spark. The biggest gift you can give them, like so many of the parents in my community have gifted their families, is to learn how to switch your lights on and hold that strong, compassionate space for them to feel it all. From Darkness to Radiance. Lights Off to Lights On. This is truly what Lights On Learning is all about – the full immersion into your inner learning landscape of what it means to unlock your human intelligence with courage, authenticity and growth.

Your family needs you to believe in them so they can believe in themselves. To do that, you may need to believe in yourself first.

This book was written for you with love because I believe you can do this.

Julia ♡

Acknowledgements

This book is the result of a twenty-year deep-dive into how we can fully express our human potential. I want to thank everyone who has interacted with my work within schools, my centres and online programmes. There are far too many to mention by name, but you know who you are. I am proud to have you as part of this unfolding adventure.

All it takes is for one person to show you what is possible. I was lucky to have a whole school community do that for me thanks to everyone involved in the enrichment events we ran through the PTA at my children's primary school. The children who grabbed the opportunities; the parents who shared their skills, talents and time; the teachers, head teacher and governors who opened the doors for us to collaborate in a unique way. We were united by a common vision for our children to shine. Without this experience, I would never have begun this adventure.

In particular, I want to thank Liz and Emmaline for saying yes to co-directing the circus and taking that leap of faith with me into the unknown. You both enabled me to understand my own creative energy and potential in a new way, and it continues to be a standout moment in my life.

I'd like to thank the pioneering families who were the first to reimagine education with me at my creative learning centre. Before I knew any of what's in this book, you tuned into my vision and trusted me. Special thanks go to Debra, Lily and Ruby – together we created something magical.

I also want to thank the families led by Nadia, Dawn and Emma who were among the first to sign up for my online community. You showed me what was possible when Lights On entered your homes. Your courage to act and lead your family away from old-school thinking paved the way for the thousands who have followed.

Thank you to all the inspiring educators I've co-created with over the years in the fifteen schools we worked with. In particular, I want to thank Carolyn Tommey, Shonogh Pilgrim and Sarah Nykoruk. You've all

ACKNOWLEDGEMENTS

shaped my deeper understanding of the obstacles we face when leading children toward excellence. You never once entertained the idea that we'd settle for anything less.

A massive thank you to everyone who's been on my team over the years. A special mention to Corinne Williams for being such a joy to play with over the years. Your ability to throw every plan up into the air and co-create magic with me in the moment has been an unimaginable gift. Thanks also to Matt Treece, my sister Jane Black, Nadia Joshua and Jo Smith, who have played their role as my right-hand man and women and made me feel safe to follow my intuition that there 'has to be a better way'. Huge thanks go to the Lights On Sparkys: Emma, Claire, Jackie, Erika, Alice, Krish, and Lights On coach Mandy for supporting so many parents to become inspiring leaders.

My book is richer thanks to the children, young people and parents who let me share their names, stories, words and insights. Thank you all for sharing your voice alongside mine.

Thanks also to my beta readers, Nadia, Rachel, Corinne, Jane, Jean (Mum) and Esme who gave me invaluable feedback on my early drafts. It feels like a long time ago, and an entirely different book has emerged as a result. I hope you are excited by how it shaped up.

Also, of course, a huge thanks goes to Mel Stephenson for bringing my concepts to life with her illustrations and to the team at Rethink Press for their patience and guidance in helping me birth my book!

A massive amount of gratitude and love goes to Esme and Seb. You were the reason I began this quest and it's been magical to watch you grow and flourish into young adults and incredible learners. You've never let me quit – ever! Every time I felt it was too hard, you reminded me of the impact we were having on the lives of many. 'Keep going, Mum,' you urged me.

To do that, I needed to find more pieces of the puzzle for my own growth. Thanks to some formidable women who changed my life forever. Dr Shannon Irvine, thanks for fast-tracking the rewiring of my brain and training me as a Master Neurocoach. Fernanda Lind, thanks for being a friend and mentor who has challenged me at every stage of my growth. You've opened my eyes to the full power, and potential, within me, for which I will be forever grateful. It was a much deeper free dive than I could ever have imagined, but wow, what a glorious one. I would also like to thank Silke Tyler for guiding me to understand the full significance of my own Radiance and what opens up through the spiritual connection to learning.

My exploration into the human creative spirit has, of course, not happened in isolation. I feel a huge amount of gratitude to the educationalists, psychologists,

ACKNOWLEDGEMENTS

scientists, philosophers, researchers, writers, creatives, spiritual teachers and entrepreneurs whose work has clearly influenced, or reinforced, my own discoveries. I work in an intuitive, hands on way, taking action then seeking evidence to back up my findings. I've found when the time was right I'd always be 'introduced' to the wisdom of others who were further along on their own path cracking the code to unlock our human potential. There are too many to name, but thank you all for the encouragement and reassurance that I was indeed on the right track.

Finally, thanks to my parents, Jean and Tim Black. Dad, even though you are no longer physically here, I talk to you regularly. Your wisdom continues to come through and I know you are proud of what we've achieved to this point. The game enters a new level now. And Mum, your support and belief in me means the world. After all, isn't that what every child wants from their parents? To hold space for them to stumble and fall as they explore how to turn their wildest dreams into reality. You and Dad have done that for me – always. That gift is the most invaluable of all. Thank you.

The Author

Julia Black, mother to two young adults and creator of Lights On Learning, is a BAFTA and Grierson nominated documentary director, social entrepreneur, educationalist and Master Neurocoach. She hosts a global community for parents who want to bring the latest thinking from neuroscience, positive psychology and passion-led learning into their homes. Her vision is of a world where all children love learning, and parents are the key to that future.

LIGHTS ON LEARNING

🌐 www.lightsonuniverse.com

☐ @thelightsonmum

🔲 www.linkedin.com/in/lightsonmum/

◎ @thelightsonmum